BEAUTIFUL AMERICAN ROSE GARDENS

BEAUTIFUL

AMERICAN ROSE

GARDENS

Mary Tonetti Dorra

PHOTOGRAPHS *by* RICHARD FELBER

CLARKSON POTTER/PUBLISHERS   NEW YORK

To my friend Julia Child, Constant and Prolific Bloomer

Published by Clarkson Potter, 201 East 50th Street, New York, New York 10022. Member of the Crown Publishing Group.
Random House, Inc. New York, Toronto, London, Sydney, Auckland
www.randomhouse.com

CLARKSON POTTER, POTTER, and colophon are registered trademarks of Random House, Inc.

Printed in China

Design by Platinum Design, Inc. NYC

Library of Congress Cataloging-in-Publication Data
Dorra, Mary Tonetti.
Beautiful American rose gardens / Mary Tonetti Dorra; photographs by Richard Felber. — 1st ed.
Includes bibliographical references and index.
1. Rose gardens—United States. I. Title.
SB411.5.U6D67   2000
635.9'33734'0973—dc21   98-43289
ISBN 0-609-60080-X

10   9   8   7   6   5   4   3   2   1

First Edition

PRECEDING PAGE: 'Olympiad' from the Krueger garden in St. Louis.

Acknowledgments

My first debt is to the Garden Club of Santa Barbara, for it encouraged me from the very beginning to lecture and write about gardens.

My heartfelt thanks go to all the garden owners and their gardeners who opened their gardens to me and gave so generously of their wisdom, time, hospitality, encouragement, and enthusiasm.

To Richard Felber, whose inspired photography captured the intrinsic beauty of the gardens.

To my agent, Helen Pratt, whose knowledge of the publishing world and unswerving guidance have been invaluable.

To Lauren Shakely, my editor at Clarkson Potter, for the energy, enthusiasm, and skills with which she enriched this project. To the Art Director at Clarkson Potter, Marysarah Quinn, and to Victoria Stamm, book designer, who highlighted so sensitively the beauty of the gardens in this book.

My gratitude goes to those who helped in finding or otherwise introducing me to the owners of the wonderful rose gardens of America: Ricky Allen, Marianne Appley, Barbara Baker, Daphne Bertero, Mrs. David Clark IV, Louise Clements, Glen Couvillion, Karen Custis, Allen Deitz, Bunny Dupont, Esther Filson, Mary Reade, Corinne Gruenwald, Virginia Scott Heard, Joanne Horskotte, Wallace Huntington, Mrs. Chandler Mashek, Rosie McIver, Wendy Minot, Mary Morgan, Cynthia Nolen, Robin Oppmann, Anne Peake, Sue Pittman, Aileen and Dorothy Roberts, Barbara Robinson, Francis Robinson, Polly Rowley, Barbara Rumsey Estele Schuleuter, Josephine Shanks, Jean Sherrill, Katie Stewart, Bess Summers, Carol Swift, and the Visiting Gardens Committees in California, Connecticut, Oregon, New Mexico, Missouri, and Texas.

I am particularly grateful to Gregg Lowery of Vintage Gardens, who shared his knowledge and let me lean on him as I ran into thorns in my meanderings through the history of the rose. Thanks also to the following for their most valuable help: Syl Arena, Dan Bifano, Dr. Thommy Cairns, Tom Carruth, Steve Jones, Ruth Knopf, Clair Martin, Rayford Reddell, Stephen Scanniello, Mike Shoup of the Antique Rose Emporium, Charles A. Walker, Jr., President of the Heritage Rose Foundation, Raleigh, North Carolina, and Bill Welch.

Special thanks to those who, in addition to the gardeners themselves and some of the above, extended gracious hospitality during the research and photographing of the book: Carolyn Amory, Nina Kivelson Auerbach, John and Barbara Avnet, Mrs. Robert Ballinger, Norma Bergerac, Mary Douglas, Wendy Foster, Helen Goddard, Millie Good, Susie and Glen Griffith, George and Corinne Gruenwald, Jill Jakes, Elena Kingsland, Sandra and Arthur Mendalo, Joseph Minton, Kirsten Peckerman, Julie and Frank Prieb, Phyllis Rowan, Susie Russell, Jean and Evritt Sherrill, the Houston, Austin, and New York Tonettis, Burnley and George Wadsworth, Robin Worcester, and Debbie Wright.

Thanks to the following rose lovers who gave generously of their time and knowledge: Drs. Geoffrey Beasley and James Sampson, Daphne Bertero, Dr. Willilam Campbell, Louise Clements, Claude and Elaine Cross, Britty Cudlipp, Dr. Fletcher Derrick, Mary Ann Green, Donna Hackman, Sarah Hammond, Beth Harrison, Bunny Hathaway, Peggy and Frank Heinsohn, Andrew and Joan Jessimen, Annabelle Josephs, Mr. and Mrs. Norm Levesque, Patty McGee, Sandra Mendalo, Peter Newton, Mrs. Charles Reed, Jr., Honey Rosenthal, Margaret Sharp, Nancy Swanson, Sir John Thouron, Peggy Valentine, Bill Welch, and Lucy Weller.

And thanks for special help along the way to the American Rose Society, Nancy Bechtel and Laura Ann Nash of the Archives of American Gardens at the Smithsonian, Marie Butler, Jaime Constance, Professor Jeff Dozier, University of California at Santa Barbara, Lou Greer, Laurie Hannah, Librarian of the Santa Barbara Botanic Garden, Wendy Minot, Senga Mortimer, Jane Radin, Michael Schultz, Susan Turner, and Virginia Gardener of VLT Gardner Books.

CONTENTS

INTRODUCTION

It is baffling to hear supposedly knowledgeable landscape architects declare that rose gardens should be sequestered apart from the general garden view because of their unsightly growth habit. Most sophisticated landscape designers today recognize that many roses have appealing form and foliage, but more important, it is simply a shame to hide away a shrub that produces perfect blossoms and arguably the world's most delicious fragrance. ❈ The twenty-four gardeners profiled here have made their roses the centerpiece—sometimes the only piece—of their gardens. From one coast to the other, from USDA Zone 4 to Zone 10, they share the same passion for roses—including their scent, their colors, their variety of forms and uses, and even the necessary evil of their protective thorns. ❈ In the last century, when Hybrid Perpetuals were crossed with Tea roses, the goal was to grow prizewinning specimens, and little attention was paid to arranging roses in a pleasing design. Planted row upon row to make identification and access easier, the old-fashioned rose bed offered little to the gardener who considered the backyard as much a place to live as to work. Today, even avid rose exhibitors arrange their collections in a way that makes the

gardens as beautiful as the individual flowers.

At least three rose species, *Rosa virginiana, R. carolina,* and *R. californica*, were native to America, and others came from Europe. The rose was such an essential plant that the Puritans imported their favorite European roses to Massachusetts. By the mid-19th century the Rose Revolution in America had reached a pitch equal to that in England and on the continent. In 1839 the most famous American rose breeder of the day, Philadelphian Robert Buist, had listed in his *American Flower Garden Directory* 250 "of the finest" among the roughly 2,000 varieties then available in the United States. Buist had propagated all the old European roses of the period and offered several American species roses as well.

So great was the demand for roses of every description that roses came to be cataloged separately from other flowers, shrubs, and trees. A. J. Downing had also contributed his list of the best roses grown in this country in his widely read book, *Cottage Residences,* which was published in 1847.

In 1872 Jackson & Perkins started their business in Newark, New York, which was later to become the biggest retail purveyor of roses by mail. Another American pioneer in the rose industry, the Conard and Jones Company of West Grove, Pennsylvania, offered as early as 1897 the first mail-order catalog. Later known as the Conard-Pyle Company, it became the largest wholesale nursery in the country, and for over 100 years has offered some of the most famous roses of all times, including the legendary 'Peace' after World War II, the popular 'Meidiland' series of Hybrid Flowering Shrubs, and more recently the 'Romantica' Shrub roses from France.

By 1900 the fifth edition of the catalog offered by the Mount Hope (Pennsylvania) Nurseries listed an impressive selection of the ongoing revolution: the compact little 3-foot Portlands, larger Bourbon shrubs with arching canes, and the Victorian favorites: Hybrid Perpetuals. The latter was by far the most popular at the time and was the first great show-rose class. It is given credit by many historians as paving the way to the Grand National Rose Show in London in 1858. Moreover, its show qualities perpetuated the craze for competitions and rose shows in general.

In the 20th century, new hybrids and developments spurred the sophistication of rose garden design. Floribundas, for example, introduced as the "Hybrid Polyantha" in 1911 in Denmark, grew taller and produced larger flowers and foliage than its parent. At the opposite end of the scale are the Miniatures. The greatest strides in the development of this highly popular class have been made in the last 20 years by the American hybridizer Ralph Moore in Visalia, California, who has produced more than 400 miniature cultivars.

Hybrid Musks, one of today's most popular landscaping rose classes, came on the scene in 1918 and were formerly called Pemberton roses after the English hybridizer Reverend Joseph Pemberton, who produced several of the earliest varieties. In the 1930s, John and Ann Bentall continued Pemberton's work, and still later, in the 1960s, this class, hardy to 15° F., vigorous, disease-resistant, and profuse-blooming, enjoyed a rebirth as it was perceived to be the perfect accent shrub in the landscape.

Other North American hybridizers have contributed to the modern Shrub class, which includes most of the Shrub roses that do not fit into the other modern classes and are not Old Garden Roses. The late Griffith Buck of Iowa left his mark in the history of the rose with his hardy, extremely disease-resistant Shrub roses, and in the 1990s the modern Shrub class continued to expand, giving birth to more hardy and increasingly disease-resistant roses such as the Rugosas and their hybrids.

The door is now open for the new millennium: already 20,000 varieties and 50 million roses are produced each year. The demand for roses will undoubtedly keep rising, and so will the number of varieties created, ever more adaptable to growing conditions, ever more fragrant and beautiful, ever better suited to delighting the rose lover. And, in a world in which man and his environment will necessarily become increasingly interdependent, the rose will be called upon to grace both the garden and the perspectives it opens upon the whole landscape. ❉

ONE

WELL BRED *in* NEW ENGLAND *and on the* ATLANTIC SEABOARD

"The Aire of New England . . . is one specially thing that commends this place . . . there is hardly a more healthful place to be found in the World that agreeth better with our English Bodyes." So said Reverend Francis Higginson in his 1629 treatise *New England's Plantation, or a Short and True Description of the Commodities and Discommodities of that Countrye.* ❋ The good English cleric may have overlooked the extremes of winter and summer in much of continental New England, as well as the considerable variation in latitude, but he may well have had in mind the soft, clean breezes blowing along the Atlantic coastline and islands off the shores of Massachusetts, Rhode Island, and New York during the rose days of summer. ❋ The island gardens on Martha's Vineyard and Nantucket, where roses have been a part of the landscape since the whaling days of the 18th century, are blessed with the good circulation and moisture of the ocean as well as the warming effects of the Gulf Stream, the warm currents of which contribute to the delightful climate so suited to "English Bodyes" as well as beautiful rose gardens. ❋ Inland in New England, on the other hand, unless only the hardiest rose varieties are grown, the harsher climate requires that other precautions be taken. As do rose gardeners in most of the interior of the northeastern United States, those of New England must protect their bushes against sub-zero temperatures by wrapping them in burlap or encasing them in insulating cones or boxes. ❋ Farther south along the Atlantic coastline, the humidity and heat of subtropical Florida create their own different problems for rose growers. Regular protection against disease and predators and, in particular, where there are nematodes in the soil, a careful choosing of only those roses grafted on Fortuniana root stock all help rosarians grow better roses. ❋ Among the most precious possessions of the early colonial settlers were their treasured copies of herbals by Gerard and other English authorities, and the slips and seeds of those roses they listed. In addition, the Pilgrim fathers took delight in the discovery of American species of roses, including *Rosa virginiana, R. palustris,* and the Climber *R. setigera,* all of which are frequently found in American rose gardens today. ❋ Just as rose growers had done since Roman times, early New Englanders grew roses for their medicinal value, for cooking, and for the perfuming of water and sachets—and for their sheer beauty. Finally, roses no doubt lifted spirits and touched hearts with remembrance of the Old Country.

PRECEDING PAGE 'QUEEN ELIZABETH' FROM THE GARDEN OF MOOR'S END ON NANTUCKET.
OPPOSITE HYBRID TEA 'FIRST PRIZE' FROM THE HORKAN GARDEN IN VIRGINIA.

SPRING BLOOMS *and* SNOW-COVERED BUSHES

MIKE LOWE IS UNDAUNTED BY THE IDEA OF INCORPORATING 4,000 ROSE BUSHES INTO HIS GARDEN IN NASHUA, NEW HAMPSHIRE, WHERE SNOW, ICE, AND SUBZERO WEATHER ARE THE NORM IN WINTER—A CLIMATE NOT USUALLY CONSIDERED IDEAL FOR THE GENUS ROSA. HIS CONFIDENCE

is well rewarded in mid-June, when his collection of old garden roses blooming in fabulous profusion is a sight to behold—and a testimony to the fact that not only do roses survive harsh winters but also many classes of the old garden roses (known familiarly as OGRs) seem to thrive on them.

The 2¼-acre property is made up of a series of garden "rooms," where Mike and Irene Lowe tend America's largest collection of the oldest rose classes: Damasks, Albas, Gallicas, Mosses, and Centifolias, as well as all the other classes that originated before the introduction of 'La France', the first Hybrid Tea, in 1867. The Lowe garden is a private garden where invited rosarians (and, by appointment, the public at large) come from all over the world to talk about and enjoy the fragrances of their roses; it is also the growing grounds and nursery for Lowe's Own-Root Roses and has been for thirty years the center for Mike Lowe's successful rose hybridizing. After his first twenty-

year-old garden was destroyed, Mike revised his thinking and began anew primarily with roses that are naturally happy in USDA Zone 4.

One of the great advantages of old roses is that they are resistant to insects and diseases and are less fussy about climate and environment than their modern hybrid cousins. Mike and Irene Lowe's roses are the best of that older group—the very opposite of the labor-intensive, pampered, often sprayed, disease-ridden, heavily pruned roses one so often incorrectly associates as being true of all roses. The Lowe roses are hardy to Zone 4—almost the upper limit of the USDA Zone map—and they require little of their owners except the basics of good horticulture: good soil preparation, proper planting, and timely watering and fertilizing.

After many years of growing and hybridizing roses, Mike says he is "cutting back to only those roses that do well here easily," which means only spring and fall spraying (and a mid-August attack on

blackspot—the number one problem in New England rose gardens). It also means very little pruning.

One of the secrets to success at Lowe's Own-Root Roses is in the very name of their nursery: most of the roses are grown on the Lowes' own rootstock, which Mike considers the most important beginning in growing healthy, disease-free roses.

The Lowes' rose garden is definitely not a rose garden in the traditional sense. Although Mike designed the garden to show off the roses in fall and spring, in summer the wildflowers upstage the roses, leaving their lush green foliage to enhance the garden for the rest of the season. Roses are integrated into the landscape, yet each one is showcased like a picture in a gallery. Each old garden rose class has its own "room," made up of beds measuring about 4 feet long and 2 feet wide, luxuriating in the well-prepared soil dug 30 inches deep with half manure and half garden loam. The number of beds in

ABOVE One of Mike Lowe's favorite views is across the "teardrop" garden from the bottom of the property. Here low-growing Polyanthas and climbing Miniatures such as 'Pink Cascade' and 'Nozomi' are interwoven with Miniature Rugosas, lilies, and yellow sedum, Mike's preferred rose companion.

RIGHT The Rambler 'White Mountains' with its glossy foliage creates a canopy of blooms over one of the many beautiful rose-lined pathways. Roses trained to climb on pillars include 'Baltimore Belle' and 'Lady Penzance' on the right.

PRECEDING PAGE 'Spencer', softly pink and scented, is at the forefront of one of the Hybrid Perpetual beds. It dates back to 1892 before this class was almost totally eclipsed by the Hybrid Tea. Among the other favorites are the little-known but vigorous vermilion 'Le Havre' and the dark crimson 'Black Prince'.

PAGE 20 Arching canes of the normally shrubby Damask 'Marie Louise', supported by a pillar, grow unusually tall in Mike's garden.

PAGE 21 In the bed that stretches to the brook in the wetlands a band of Miniature Rugosas and dwarf Shrub roses grow with a climbing pink 'Albertine' used as a ground cover.

each room varies according to the magnitude of the collection and the size of the rose bush itself.

Once a year, the Lowes' magnificent collection of Centifolias, or cabbage roses, is in bloom and this show alone—a Redouté painting come to life—is worth a trip to the Lowe garden. Mike grows twenty-seven varieties of this fairly rare class and sixty-eight varieties of its sport, the equally rare Moss rose that ranges from white to light pink to purple-red with the striped 'Oeillet Panachée' right in the middle. The buds, stems, and sepals of the Moss roses are covered with light green prickly tufts, giving them their mossy look and thus their name.

Strong vertical accents are Mike's ·favorite way to show his old garden roses. Sometimes the Hybrid Musks stand alone in isolated splendor like tall, elegant chalices of champagne (both pink and white), encouraged to bubble up over the top in huge mounds of frothy blooms. They and the splendid pink *Hybrid Multifolia* 'Tausendschön' are trained to climb telephone poles reaching as high as 10 to 15 feet. Others, including Bourbons, are supported by 10-foot-high treated-wood pillars with circular crossbars placed at regular 1-foot intervals alternating north/south and east/west for the elevated explosion of blooms all the way up the pillar.

In explaining his unconventional yet beautifully arranged collection, Mike says, "We are freer in the United States in designing our rose gardens. We don't always work in pairs or in threes. We aren't bound by tradition. In our garden, for example, we have several focal points, but everything outside the focal point is the splash. That is what I like—the splash. I wanted the design to be based on the formality of the French without its being so strict." Because of both the staggered blooming season and the position of the various beds, the garden rooms cannot be viewed all at once. The rooms are connected by grassy paths that wind through the open spaces, among the trees and beneath arching canes of carefully placed hardy Climbers.

One of the most beautiful parts of the garden is a tract of marshland that has been transformed into raised beds that not only solve the drainage problem but are aesthetically pleasing as well. Over the years, the Lowes have added roses in this reclaimed wetlands next to a meandering brook at the edge of the garden. Here, dwarf Rugosas and Species roses fit naturally into the landscape with cattails and marsh grasses. The soft green foliage of the Rugosas echoes the intense green of the grassy paths and the pines, locusts, and willow trees.

Throughout the garden, the Lowes' rose season is almost symphonic. From the first blooms of Species roses in the second week of May to the last Rugosas in the fall, the combinations of color and scent crescendo to their peak in mid-June and then fade slowly toward midsummer. A few roses return to offer unexpected "last of the season" grace notes, even after the first frost.

Mike also grows those other old garden roses that came about as a result of

OEILLET PANACHÉE

Moss

One of the most unusual of the Mosses because of its richly striped blush-pink and crimson multipetaled flowers, 'Oeillet Panachée' (*Rosa centifolia muscosa*), like most in its class, is once-blooming, fragrant, and distinguished by the bristle-like glands covering the sepals, receptacles, and stems (thus the "Moss" in its common name).

The beautifully mossed buds and striped blooms make this cultivar especially effective when placed alone as a specimen. In a mixed border in early summer, it is a show-stopper, and when not in bloom it fades gently into the background. Since it rarely reaches beyond 3 feet in cold climates, it makes a good container rose. In warmer regions it can reach up to 6 feet. Of all the Mosses it is the least affected by mildew and blackspot and in warmer climates by powdery mildew. Its fragrance is light and fresh.

Closely aligned with the history of the Cabbage Rose, Mosses are known to have been growing in France as early as 1696. 'Oeillet Panachée', introduced in 1888, and other Mosses are classified as Old Garden Roses, although most were not introduced until the mid-19th century, when they became Victorian favorites. Mosses first appeared as Damask and Centifolia sports, each bringing different growth habits to the class—tall and upright from the Damask and more bushy with arching canes from the Centifolia.

ROSES ARE INTEGRATED into the landscape, yet each one is showcased like a picture in a gallery.

the introduction of the Bourbon class during the 19th-century explosion of rose hybridizing in Europe. This class made rose history on the Île de Bourbon in the Indian Ocean (now Réunion) in 1817, when a natural cross occurred between an everblooming China rose and the cold-hardy European Damask rose. Happily, the result was a class of *remontant,* or repeat-blooming, roses known for profuse blooms in early summer and sporadic repeat blooming until fall.

Mike's garden—with his ninety varieties of Bourbons—includes many not even listed in the official rose list put out by the American Rose Society, *Modern Roses 10.* The Bourbons, along with sister classes (Portlands, Hybrid Perpetuals, and Teas) begat from the same imported roses of China, enjoy their own designated area in the Lowe garden, where they climb and swirl and mound into various shades from scarlet to mauve to pink to snow white. Some of the most popular of the Bourbons, both in Mike's garden and elsewhere among old garden rose fanciers, are the elegantly cupped 'Louise Odier', the striped 'Variegata di Bologna', and the strongly scented 'Madame Isaac Pereire'.

Many of these above-mentioned antique classes were introduced even after 1867, the date ascribed to the first modern rose. Yet they are still called old garden roses (OGRs) because the classes themselves predate that first modern Hybrid Tea.

Mike's love of roses in full bloom does not mean he ignores the other seasons. Mike understands, as do other advocates of the American Gardening Style, that a truly American garden must be beautiful at all seasons—even in winter. He consciously planned the garden to show off its winter bone structure, the bush and shrub silhouettes, raised beds, and carefully placed trees for accents of vertical height and mass, as well as the 4-foot-long snow-covered boxes made of Homosote (a composite board) and built to cover the entire length of the bed. The garden is an enchanting sight as frosted hips of orange, gold, yellow, and cherry red stand out against the snow-covered bushes in the long view from the kitchen window, framed by pine boughs heavy with snow. In order to preserve the stunning natural view even in winter, the chosen roses are hardy enough to go without "winterizing"—that is, without the rose cones and protective boxes used for the more tender roses in other parts of the garden.

"Although many OGRs bloom only once in the early summer, there are literally thousands of blooms, while a typical Hybrid Tea will produce only about twelve to fourteen blossoms a year. Most Hybrid Teas won't survive the winter here in New Hampshire, while the old garden roses are practically carefree. That's why I grow them."

The most dramatic view of the garden is from the bottom near the wetlands. Reached by following the paths through several rooms and the open area encircled with Species roses and edged with New Hampshire fieldstones, this viewpoint looks back at the elongated bed Mike calls his "teardrop garden" filled with lilies and his favorite rose companions, yellow sedums, used as fillers between low-growing Miniature roses and early Polyantha roses. Here, Mike keeps weeds under control with a few Large-flowered Climbers such as 'Albertine' and 'Rosarium Ueteresen' used ingeniously as ground covers. Occasionally a hardy compact 3-foot Portland is nestled in, just to remind us that this is a rose historian's garden and the 'Duchess of Portland' should not be forgotten. ❈

"WE ARE FREER in the United States in designing our rose gardens. We don't always work in pairs or in threes. We aren't bound by tradition."

LEFT Part of the charm of the Lowe garden is the seemingly random mixture of old roses and new. Here a telephone pole with crossbars at intervals makes the climb a little easier for a climbing red "splash"—an experimental rose called simply 'Modern 6910'—next to 'Lowe's Eglantine #1' and separated by the luscious pink Alba, 'Blush Hip', all of which are offered by mail through Lowe's Own Root Roses.

BELOW 'James Veitch', a dwarf repeat-blooming Moss raised in 1864 by Philippe-Victor Verdier, is fragrant and covered with the glandular growth that resembles moss. Today, as in the Victorian era, Moss roses are appreciated as much for their moss-covered buds as for their multipetaled, fully opened blooms.

A WHALER'S WIFE'S GARDEN

BY THE END OF THE 18TH CENTURY AND WELL INTO THE 19TH, THE WINDSWEPT ISLAND OF NANTUCKET, 22 MILES OFF THE COAST OF CAPE COD, WAS HOME FOR PROSPEROUS, ENTERPRISING NEW ENGLANDERS SEEKING THEIR FORTUNES IN WHALING. THE MOST SUCCESSFUL OF

those were Joseph Starbuck and his chief competitor, Jared Coffin, both of whom knew not only the value of whale oil but also how to spend fortunes wisely and beautifully. In 1827, Jared Coffin built for his wife Moor's End, a conservative yet handsome brick house—the first on Nantucket—with plans and bricks imported from England.

By 1898, when Henry Bigelow Williams bought Moor's End, the whaling industry had long since expired, many of the Starbucks and Coffins had left Nantucket, and the island had settled into an economic depression. Nevertheless, it was Bigelow who planned the garden, built its walls, and installed its first boxwood and roses.

Today, strolling through the 100-year-old garden at Moor's End, now owned by Marilyn Whitney and cared for by Dieter Schmidt, the gardener, one is reminded that collecting roses with a passion is not limited to the 20th century or to whalers' wives in Nantucket or to empresses and kings.

The architect Fiske Kimball, who was responsible for some of the previous restorations of Moor's End, described the home as belonging to "the Nantucket not of the early struggle but of the height of whaling prosperity, when the owners lived a life of dignity and elegance." Since 1986, Marilyn Whitney, who considers herself the "custodian of the future" at Moor's End, has been restoring the house and gardens to their original quiet elegance, repairing and adding appropriate garden structures where nature had taken its toll and the disappearance of old Dutch elms had opened the garden to more light. Today, with the help of Dieter, who oversees more than 600 rose bushes in the garden, Marilyn devotes countless hours to the research and preservation of this important early-19th-century connection with Nantucket's past. "When I walk over the worn threshold at Moor's End I am reminded of all the people who have come and gone here for almost 200 years. Someone had cared

enough to begin this project and to make something special of it, and it's a responsibility and a privilege to be able to take what they did and to build from that."

In the garden today, the original formal parterres are filled with a splendid collection of modern roses—mostly Hybrid Teas, although 'Queen Elizabeth', the first great Grandiflora, towers majestically over all. It is one of the few bushes dating back to the pre-Whitney/Schmidt era, offering testimony to its winter hardiness. The boxwood (*Buxus sempervirens*), one of the garden's chief assets, mostly dates to the time of Henry Bigelow Williams. As the property declined over the years, the box had been allowed to grow far too tall (up to 8 feet) and far too wide for people to walk comfortably in the garden. Cut back by two-thirds, the hedges then had to be supplemented with 150 new boxwood bushes to fill in the gaps. Today, annual pruning keeps the boxwood at a healthy and handsome 3 feet, allowing

ABOVE 'All That Jazz' is one of the most vibrant of the new hardy landscape Shrub roses of the 1990s. Before completely opening to reveal luscious golden yellow stamens, sprays of coral-salmon buds and large, cupped, semi-double blossoms dazzle the eye and delight the gardener with disease-resistant foliage.

RIGHT The rose-bedecked fronts of Nantucket's Main Street houses have become one of the signatures of the island's charm since the 18th century. Here the modern climber 'New Dawn' signals the arrival of summer.

PRECEDING PAGE In 1898, by the time the garden at Moor's End was laid out, old roses were no longer in fashion. 'La France', the first modern rose or Hybrid Tea, had been introduced in 1867 and would eclipse all other roses for almost a century. The 100-year-old boxwood had to be cut back by two thirds when Marilyn Whitney acquired the property in 1986.

the structure to remain formal yet leaving a clear vista for garden visitors to admire the roses.

Beginning his annual rose care in April, Dieter removes the protective mulch of seaweed. Gathered on the beach and carefully placed in late fall, the seaweed offers natural minerals as well as winter protection. Dieter prefers seaweed to commercial mulches "because it lets the ground breathe and the climate here is mild enough not to have to wrap the roses." The dead wood and any roses that failed to survive the Nantucket winter are then removed and canes are cut back drastically, to just about a foot or two tall. In the first of three annual feedings, Espoma, an organic fertilizer, is watered into the soil. Six weeks later, the roses get a second feeding, this time with an Ortho systemic fertilizer. The final feeding, again Espoma, is usually in July because Dieter has learned by experience that, if done any later, the resulting blooms will surely be killed by the frost.

Dieter is conscientious in his diligent garden housekeeping: petals are almost never allowed to touch the ground—and Japanese beetles are individually hunted on a daily basis in the early-morning hours and dropped into a jar filled with kerosene. "When you see a little black hole on the side of a blossom you know they are inside. They are easy to pick when it is early in the morning, before the sun has warmed them up." Likewise, blackspot leaves are carefully removed by hand so that they never contaminate the soil. This common rose disease often persists in spite of Dieter's early-season preventive spraying (of Funginex alternated with Benomyl) applied even before the problems become apparent, when the young leaves first appear.

The short-season rose garden is tended for the delight it brings to many Nantucket visitors throughout the summer months, usually for the benefit of local charities when the garden is open to the public. In addition, Dieter's pruning throughout the summer ensures masses of beautiful cut roses that the Whitneys take pleasure in offering to their many friends. By late October, the Nantucket nights have become so cold that all but the hardiest roses have called an end to the season. ✳

QUEEN ELIZABETH

Grandiflora

Produced by E. Lammerts, an American hybridizer, 'Queen Elizabeth' has won more awards than most modern roses including, in 1978, the World Federation of Rose Societies' "World's Favorite Rose." While English rosarians recognized it as being uniquely taller than the "Cluster-flowered" roses of the day, they did not believe it merited the establishment of a new class, the Grandiflora. For them (and some American rosarians as well) this medium-pink statuesque (up to 7 feet) should be classified as "Cluster-flowered" or as a Floribunda.

English horticulturist Peter Beales writes that 'Queen Elizabeth' achieved a popularity as a hedge rose almost to the exclusion of all others. When grown on its own root stock it is hardy and disease resistant. Its fragrance is another asset. Where tall roses are needed—for example, to stand majestically above high boxwood borders—'Queen Elizabeth' is an ideal choice.

Grandifloras should not be pruned as much as Hybrid Teas or Floribundas for, as rosarian Ray Reddell explains, 'Queen Elizabeth' "will spend most of the growing season reaching the height at which she blooms comfortably." His own 'Queen Elizabeths' reach 8 or 9 feet and are pruned only by half. Disbudding should be limited as the impressive sprays on tall canes are this rose's spectacular feature and ideal for the back of the border.

PROFUSION *in the* SEA BREEZES

PRECISELY AT THE END OF MARCH EACH YEAR, DAVID AND HELGA DAWN LEAVE THEIR FLORIDA HOME AND RETURN TO LONG ISLAND FOR ABOUT TEN DAYS TO FULFILL A COMMITMENT THAT BEGAN MORE THAN THIRTY YEARS AGO. ALTHOUGH IT GIVES THE DAWNS THEMSELVES MUCH PLEASURE,

the annual March trip is not a pleasure trip in the usual sense. The Dawns have a serious job to do: pruning the 2,000 rose bushes and inevitably planting some new ones at their summer home, aptly called La Roseraie.

Helga and David Dawn's dedication to growing such a large number of roses strictly for their own enjoyment is unparalled and their achievement is remarkable. Not only has their knowledge and passionate interest in the art of rose culture earned them the respect of rosarians all over the world but also their humility in this scientific-artistic area is as rare as it is appealing.

Their ongoing, hands-on experimenting for over sixty years is often highly scientific as they take advantage of research on pruning, fertilizing, and watering by rose hybridizers here, in Germany, and in England. But it is their own beautifully designed 2½-acre garden that earns the admiration of every visitor. The Dawns' garden is laid out in border-garden style, yet the borders are not typically perennials but are entirely of roses. Numerous beds flank the large grassy lawn and are devoted to specific classes of roses, including antique, modern Hybrid Teas, Floribundas, Polyanthas, Miniatures, English, Rugosas, a 1998 bed for the newest variety of modern Shrub roses—the Romantica series produced by the French grower Meilland—and finally a particularly impressive collection of Climbers. The latter are trained to form garlands, pillars, towers, and even a "bridal wreath" on an umbrella-shaped *tuteur*. The beds, always carefully planned according to small, medium, and tall bushes so that everything can be shown to best advantage, host a glorious profusion of intermingling colors in a healthy horticultural environment. The garden peaks in June but offers an almost unbelievable display from late May to October. How, one wonders, can it be achieved by only two gardeners with one helper?

David Dawn and his German-born wife, Helga, attribute part of their success to having chosen the hardiest roses for their subzero winters, many of which are Shrub and Climbing varieties of the Kordes group. In 1919, Wilhelm Kordes, a passionate German rosarian, started a family nursery, Kordes Sohne, in Sparrieshoop, Germany, with the help of his two sons. Kordes is the only rosarian who has been honored by having a rose species named after him: *Rosa kordesii*. Although the Dawns grow the Kordes rose 'Iceberg', the most popular rose of all time, there are others in the Dawn garden that are perhaps less well known but equally worthy of praise: 'Dortmund', 'Sparrieshoop', and the Explorer series from Canada, all of which have Kordes in their histories. "That Canadian series is so strong I put one of them, 'William Baffin', right where the wind blows through. It can reach twenty degrees below freezing here and that one, along with 'John Cabot', another hardy member of the Explorer series, never seems to mind the wind and cold." Not only are the

ABOVE 'Helga', a Floribunda that David esteems as one of the most beautiful whites, has been almost discontinued for lack of demand, and has been replaced by 'Iceberg', a Kordes rose that is the most popular rose in American landscapes.

RIGHT A dramatic range of pillar roses lining the pergola are, from left to right, the deep pink 'Rosarium Ueteresen' next to a white clematis, the red 'Hamburger Phoenix', the yellow 'Lichtkönigin Lucia', and finally the brilliant orangy-red 'Spectacular'.

PRECEDING PAGE David Dawn believes all colors mix well in nature. His planting scheme is controlled by the height of the roses rather than anything else. Shown here the yellow Miniature 'Rise 'n' Shine' and behind it the low-growing Shrub rose 'Carefree Beauty', with its hardy double medium-pink blooms born abundantly on sprays.

Kordes descendants very hardy and vigorous but they have the repeat blooms and glossy, deep green foliage one has come to identify with those roses.

But Kordes shrubs are not the only members of the Dawn's rose family. "I love Climbers," says David with characteristic enthusiasm, and he has several favorites, also Kordes roses, that they first saw in Germany in the 1970s. Today the Dawns order their new additions from Pickering Nurseries in Canada. The Dawns' 50-foot-long by 15-foot-high pergola, which they added fifteen years after the garden was begun, is mostly covered with Kordes Climbers. Its rose-covered ceiling covers a walkway underneath so that one is enveloped by strongly perfumed blossoms. These include the deep pink 'Rosarium Ueteresen'; 'Hamburger Phoenix', a little-known but spectacular red; the yellow-flowered 'Lichtkönigin Lucia'; 'Morgengruss' ('Morning Greeting'), whose breathtaking light pink blossoms with a tinge of yellow-orange are extremely fragrant; and red 'Illusion', a Shrub rose that the Dawns have trained as a climber.

The Dawns have also 'Dortmund', mentioned earlier, another climber classified as a Shrub rose, growing up one of the six 10-foot-high pillars David designed to support climbing roses and to connect the garlands. On another pillar, 'Lavender Lassie', a favorite Hybrid Musk of Kordes parentage, perfumes the garden most of the day with lilac-pink blooms.

Many Ramblers, another huge class of climbing rose that is well represented at La Roseraie, offer numerous once-blooming flowers that continue for several weeks and almost always provide a delightful fragrance. 'Albéric Barbier' and 'Seagull' are among the favorite Ramblers grown on 10-foot pillars. 'American Pillar', another successful cold-tolerant Rambler, blooms along the 125-foot chain garlands "like a string of beads" two weeks after the mid-June peak and adds dramatically to the continuous showstopping display.

'Paul's Himalayan Musk Rambler', one of the most popular Ramblers in the country, typically grows up to 30 feet every year in the Dawn garden, simultaneously camouflaging the trunks and branches of the property's dead pines and screening the garden from the neighbors' houses. The dead trunk of a black pine serves as support for two very successful tree climbers: the beautiful 'Kiftsgate', a Species climber (*R. filipes*) with clusters of white blossoms, and its salmon-pink Rambler offspring, 'Treasure Trove', whose glossy foliage fills in nicely.

Not content simply to share their garden with each other, the Dawns educate other amateur rose growers through their frequent lectures over the years and the guided tours of their garden. They have earned the distinguished Garden Club of America Jane Righter Rose Medal award "for their outstanding devotion to rose culture, as demonstrated by their magnificent rose garden which they generously share, along with their experience and knowledge, with novices and experts alike." ❈

LINDA CAMPBELL

Hybrid Rugosa (Shrub)

When David Dawn planted 'Linda Campbell' in a location where the winds whipped through from the Long Island Sound and the temperatures dipped regularly to the lowest point in the garden, he was testing the rose's reputation for hardiness. This large double-bloomed, repeat-flowering, disease-resistant beauty sports healthy, semiglossy foliage and luminous medium red blooms that cover the 7 by 7-foot shrub. The importance of the class, however, is as the provider of root stock for the hardiest roses of today: Kordes and the Canadian Explorer series.

In 1990, when Ralph Moore produced the exceedingly successful and beautiful 'Linda Campbell', he named it for a Denver friend, a respected rosarian who was as vibrant and popular as the rose in her name has come to be.

Suzanne Verrier points out in her definitive book on Rugosas, *Rosa Rugosa,* that in addition to its hardiness (to as cold a region as Zone 2), 'Linda Campbell' has impressive versatility. Some varieties are used as a ground cover, others as a soil-holding bank-retainer, as a dense thorny protective barrier, or quite simply, as in the Dawn garden, as an eye-catching specimen plant. While many of the Hybrid Rugosas do not have the colorful large hips of the true Rugosas, most of their foliage turns from dark or light green into beautiful fall tones.

OPPOSITE One of Helga Dawn's beautifully composed bouquets using various shades of pale yellow, apricot, and peach Hybrid Teas. The largest in the front of the heirloom Victorian vase is 'Medallion', and others to be noted are the apricot-tinged 'French Lace' and 'Elina', whose blooms change from yellow to pale ivory.

RIGHT Formally clipped hedges are in sharp contrast to the blowsy feeling of the Dawns' collection of English Shrub roses. Here 'Constance Spry', the first of David Austin's English roses, introduced in 1961, reaches almost as high (10 feet) as the lowest branches of a neighboring sycamore tree. Its pale pink globe blossoms cover the bush once early in the season and the profusion of multipetaled blooms offer an intense, unforgettable fragrance.

BELOW Experts agree there is no more perfect climbing rose than 'Royal Sunset', which was introduced in 1960 by Jackson & Perkins yet still today holds its 9.2 ARS rating. Here hundreds of hardy, fragrant apricot blooms provide a magnificent backdrop reaching upward of 6 feet. The large cupped, semi-double flowers fade with age to an equally beautiful yet softer blush of apricot blends. Other Large-flowered Climbers continue the cyclorama of brilliant colors into the distance.

FOLLOWING PAGES

LEFT Floribundas are among the most effectively used roses in the Dawn landscape. Shown here planted closely together are the yellow 'Sunsprite', then orangey 'Redgold', deep red 'Europeana', and the white 'Saratoga'—all favorites of David and Helga Dawn. Pillar roses in the background are connected by swags of 'American Pillar'. Branches of a tree that died several years ago provide a natural trellis for Paul's Himalayan Musk, one of the Dawn Ramblers that that reaches for the sky.

RIGHT Even though the awesome climbing roses surrounding the lawn are what most visitors remember about La Roseraie, the lavish display of the Floribunda beds is breathtaking. Here the luxuriant curving sweep of 'Gene Boerner' introduces the beds that continue a colorful line of medium-tall Floribundas beneath the climbers.

MANY RAMBLERS offer numerous
once-blooming flowers that continue for
several weeks and almost always provide
a delightful fragrance.

An ENGLISH GEM in PALM BEACH

WHEN JOANNE DAYTON FIRST SAW THE CREAMY WHITE DAVID AUSTIN ROSE 'SWAN' AT THE CHELSEA FLOWER SHOW IN THE MID-1970S, SHE THOUGHT IT "THE MOST BEAUTIFUL ROSE IN LONDON." IT INSPIRED HER TO BRING IT AND AS MANY OTHER ENGLISH ROSES (AS THEY ARE

generally called) as she could find in order to add them to the collection already growing in her Palm Beach garden. A regular visitor to England who was among the first to recognize how beautiful this new hybrid group would be in American gardens, Joanne also found that growing them in southern Florida is not for the easily discouraged.

"I was always taken by Gertrude Jekyll and by Vita Sackville-West's gardens at Sissinghurst . . . all those rooms I think are charming and, although I didn't copy them, the rooms served as an inspiration for our own garden. The roses were very important to me, and in designing the garden I wanted to look down on roses in a patterned garden from my bedroom on the second floor. "Ideally," she added, "I would like my rose garden to be filled with David Austins all just 3 feet high. But in this climate it is almost impossible to keep them that way."

In 1976, after buying their Palm Beach house, Alan and Joanne Dayton

thought seriously about the garden they wanted. They asked an old friend and architect, Henry Melich, to help with the design. In recognition of her Anglophilia, he brought in the English design firm Colefax and Fowler, which had designed the interior of the house. Together they laid out the gardens in a pattern of interlocking circles. As Melich explained, "The front garden was a cooperative effort. We all worked on it together, but the roses are of Joanne's choosing. I put in the background and the Daytons painted it in." The last member of the team is Jodi Lowe, the Palm Beach rosarian who maintains the garden and as many as fifty others in the area.

The 40 by 40-foot garden is set apart from the street by a wall of ficus that follows the metal frame Henry Melich devised to enclose the garden and provide the backbone for the hedge, "just to keep it tidy." The interlocking circles are outlined by narrow bands of old bricks, emphasizing the circular pattern. Some

of the circles are centered with topiary gardenia trees clipped into perfect round puffs. Four other circles balance the small garden at each side, with four terra-cotta pots planted with citrus trees and underskirted with petunias or lantana. They serve to anchor the swirls of perfectly maintained grassy lawn forming irregular "S" shapes throughout the garden and connecting the entire mosaic with the most graceful curves. In the four corners, the clipped balls echo the perfectly rounded gardenia shrubs and the central focal point of the garden, where a circle of gravel sets off four still smaller gardenia balls that encircle a dramatic spiky agave succulent.

As a result of the collaborative efforts of architect, owner, and maintenance gardener, not only is the garden design one of the most remarkable in the country but also the plantings themselves are a horticultural tour de force: English roses in subtropical Zone 10. Joanne loves looking down on the mosaic pattern of the garden, but at the

same time she wishes the roses were in proper proportion within the 16-inch-high ilex borders. But to most visitors the garden is unparalleled and the roses, in particular, are beautifully grown.

In Florida, if roses are not grafted on Fortuniana rootstock, the nematodes in the soil usually succeed in destroying the root system in less than two years. Fortuniana was a popular Italian under-stock at one time and is particularly well adapted to poor sandy soils and hot climates. When grafted onto Fortuniana stock the Austin roses will survive, but Joanne Dayton has found in the warm Florida climate that they "reach to the sky and the few blooms they do produce are at the end of very tall canes."

For the past twenty years, the Daytons have enjoyed one of the earliest of the Austin roses, the beautiful 'Canterbury' of 1969, which for them in Florida is quite different from elsewhere in the United States and England. It sometimes opens to rosy-pink single flowers with striking yellow-gold stamens; in cooler weather and with additional manure, it grows with the usual multi-petaled look. When the Daytons bought the rose they thought it was 'Belle Story', which may have been mislabeled, but today the beautiful stamens and soft

shallow-cupped form have led experts to identify it as 'Canterbury'. 'Hero', with the old-fashioned look of cupped blooms in a strong lush pink, is another favorite that also has very prominent gold stamens. Walking through the garden one morning, Alan Dayton pointed out a glorious shade of apricot in the petals of 'Tamora'. "By tonight," he reminded his visitors, "the color will have changed dramatically; only a suggestion of the apricot tint will remain because of the sun."

In addition to the David Austins, Joanne has selected a few choice Hybrid Teas that do well in the Florida climate, such as 'Bride's Dream', and 'Double Delight'. Floribundas with an old rose look, such as the rosy-pink 'Emily', also do well here. In the Dayton rose garden, one might also find a few Bermuda Mystery roses and Teas such as 'Anna Oliver' and 'Mme. Joseph Schwartz'.

This many-faceted jewel in its lush tropical setting, with immaculately trimmed parterres, healthy boxed citrus that the Sun King would have coveted for his Versailles garden, and the ongoing success of growing English roses in Florida, is one of America's truly outstanding gardens. ❋

CANTERBURY

Shrub

Some experts, including Dr. Tommy Cairns, president-elect of the American Rose Society and editor of *Modern Roses 10*, say the Shrub rose group, developed by David Austin in the 1950s, should be called the "Hybrid Shrub" class, since all are crosses between old garden roses and modern roses. Others refer to the group as Modern Shrubs, English Roses, or simply as David Austins.

'Canterbury', first offered in 1969, is an early offspring of 'Constance Spry', David Austin's first English Rose. Its mildly fragrant, elegant, almost single-petaled blooms hold beautifully as cut flowers if picked when the buds are about to unfurl. The rose-pink blooms have a hint of yellow at the base, casting a golden amber halo around its bright yellow stamens. Although 'Canterbury' is sometimes hard to find, its blooms make it one of the most outstanding roses for the garden.

Its dark green foliage is only mildly disease-resistant in most of the United States, but in the Daytons' subtropical Palm Beach garden, where rose-growing is a challenge for most gardeners, spraying for rust and mildew is a necessity.

In warm climates, 'Canterbury' grows a little taller than it does in cool climates, where it can be expected to reach only 2½ feet and equally wide. Because of its even shrubby growth it is particularly effective as a beautiful specimen shrub.

OPPOSITE A mosaic-like jewel, the Dayton garden is set within an ilex hedge and made up of parterres of rose beds banded by grassy swirls and ribbons of brick paths.

PRECEDING PAGE 'Hero' is one of the purest pinks in the Daytons' David Austin collection.

FOLLOWING PAGES, LEFT 'Caramella', a lovely though somewhat hard to find Meilland Hybrid Tea, thrives in Florida, Texas, and southern California. RIGHT Seen at a distance, with the towering palm in the background, the Dayton garden looks both elegant and exotic.

NOT ONLY IS THE GARDEN DESIGN one of the most remarkable in the country, but also the plantings themselves are a horticultural tour de force: English roses in subtropical Zone 10.

TWO

CONFEDERATE ROSES *in the* GRAND MANNER

Eighteenth-century southerners must have been as rugged as the native American roses, *Rosa virginiana* and *R. carolina*, their forebears found when settling the first American colony at Jamestown in 1607, after earlier frustrating attempts to colonize the New World. Famine, disease, pirate ambushes, and Indian raids plagued them unmercifully. But the clipper ships that took the rice and tobacco back to England returned with the latest botanical innovations. Horticultural collections and beautiful gardens of the large rice and tobacco plantations soon reflected the prosperity of the landed gentry in the South. The South added its own chapter to the history of the rose. In Charleston in 1802, a Carolina rice farmer named John Champneys bred one of the four China studs, 'Parson's Pink China', with a musk, *R. moschata,* producing 'Champneys' Pink Cluster', the first rose in the first American rose class: the Noisette. Perhaps as a token of friendship, Champneys had given some seeds of his rose to a South Carolinian French friend, Philippe Noisette. Philippe, in turn, sent the best seedlings back to his nurseryman brother in France, Louis Noisette, after whom the class is named despite its American origins. Louis honored the

American rice farmer by naming his first imported seedling 'Champneys Pink Cluster' and followed it with his own hybrid, 'Blush Noisette', generally considered one of the oldest in the class. ❀ With the Civil War, the devastation of the southern plantations was almost total. Yet a few of the mansions survived, along with their grounds landscaped with magnificent oaks, pines, magnolias, and cypresses dripping with moss, and other vestiges of the grandeur of the Old South. ❀ Beginning in the 19th century and continuing to this day, many of the crumbling halls and manor houses along with their gardens have been restored or completely rebuilt. Most enjoyed a river view, and though many of the gardens were laid out in a formal manner—often with the traditional boxwood frame—their plantings were lush and freshly informal. In some cases today, the sweet scents of *Daphne odora*, magnolia blossoms, and roses help recapture the romantic atmosphere of the antebellum South. ❀ Noisettes, along with their hybrid offspring Tea Noisettes and two other old rose classes—Chinas and Teas—that came about as a result of breeding with the repeat-blooming four China studs settled pleasingly into the hot climate of the South. All three of these tender repeat-blooming classes, with their loose, airy foliage and relaxed charm, were particularly appropriate both in the early-19th-century southern gardens and in the reconstructed plantation gardens of today. Even the style in which these everblooming roses grew was very much apart from the European gardens, where all was usually orderly perfection. The rose gardens of the South expressed the same overflowing hospitality as did the plantation owners.

BLUE RIBBONS *in* HUNT COUNTRY

"MY WHOLE LIFE I WANTED TO BE A FARMER," SAYS ANN-MARI HORKAN OF CLEREMONT FARM IN VIRGINIA. ANN-MARI, WHO WAS BORN IN SWEDEN, IS NOT STRICTLY A FARMER, ALTHOUGH SHE AND HER HUSBAND, GEORGE, A LAWYER, HAVE RECEIVED AN AWARD FROM THE VIRGINIA

Beef Industry for their Angus beef. She is also active arranging flowers for the local church, co-chairing the annual Garden Club of America meeting for 600 attendants, winning blue ribbons for her roses in competitive shows, or preserving Cleremont, an 18th-century home listed on the Virginia Landmarks Register as one of the oldest in Loudoun County. Whatever she does, it is with efficiency and style.

As for Ann-Mari's 247 garden roses, they are grown with the same enthusiasm, research, and discipline that she applies to her unlimited roles in the home and community. "I designed my country garden from the memory of my grandmother's island garden outside Stockholm," she explains. "It had many perennials mixed in with the roses and a rather English look." In this Virginia country garden, the views of the Blue Ridge Mountains are an important addition to the garden's appeal.

On the two sides nearest the main house, the garden is enclosed by field-stone walls—one of Cleremont's several historic connections with colonial days. The ten rectangular beds within the enclosures are carefully arranged islands in the middle of a large sea of lawn. Within the islands, roses are planted 24 inches apart in neat rows. The center of the lawn is emphasized by a square oasis of apple and pear trees, both serving as a shady place of repose between garden chores and lending an element of country charm.

As Ann-Mari's rose collection grows each year, space is shared in the neighboring six long, thin beds (originally cut from the lawn and designated solely for perennials) with the campanulas, anemones, iris, delphinium, and Shasta daisies (*Chrysanthemum maximum*)—all good rose companions.

Trained as an interior designer, Ann-Mari appreciates contrasting textures, combining the rough fieldstone walls with the soft, gracefully arched branches of her Shrub and Climbing roses. Here and there she has positioned one of the specimens in her modern Shrub rose collection along the attractive wooden fence that separates the garden on two sides from the pastures. Artfully placed, the roses enhance, rather than interrupt, the magnificent view of the Virginia hunt country beyond.

Ann-Mari's real garden passion is not so much the design as the study and activity of horticulture. Her efforts are rewarded when the successive displays of perfectly grown roses begin coming in mid-May. Among her triumphs are glorious sprays of the dependable Floribundas 'Gene Boerner' or 'Dicky' or of 'Tournament of Roses', a prizewinner for Ann-Mari and others in the Grandiflora class throughout the country. She has had success at the show table with her favorite Hybrid Teas, 'Pristine', 'Gold Medal', 'First Prize', 'Sweet Surrender', and 'Double Delight', grown for their perfect form and outstandingly large blooms. But it is for her well-groomed sprays of 'China Doll'

LEFT Artfully arranged, the roses at Claremont enhance rather than interrupt the magnificent view of the Virginia Hunt country beyond. Grassy paths frame the ten rose beds where Hybrid Teas are planted 24 inches apart in neat rows. A fieldstone wall on the right is typical of this part of Virginia and links the property with its colonial roots.

PRECEDING PAGE From coast to coast one of the most popular David Austin roses is 'Othello' whose cupped clear red blooms are extremely fragrant. Shown here, the upright shrub is covered with large repeat blooming blossoms. It blooms more profusely than its parent, 'The Squire', another gorgeous red.

IRRESISTIBLE

Miniature

A Miniature is generally defined by the size of its bloom, not the size of the bush. Strictly speaking, to be correctly classified as a Miniature the bush should be under 2 feet, but some of the highest ARS-rated roses (big or little) and the most frequent prizewinners in the Miniature class are 'Jean Kenneally' (9.5) and 'Irresistible' (9.4), both of which grow to 4 feet. Both of these jewel-like exhibition roses were produced by Dee Bennett of Tiny Petals Nursery.

'Irresistible' is treasured for its profusion of long-stemmed, high-centered white blooms that have a blush of pink at the center. Ann-Mari Horkan grows a small collection of them with other Miniatures next to the entry of her guest house. They can also be used as an attractive edging or as fillers in a perennial bed, or, where space is limited, on a balcony or small terrace. Miniatures can be effectively grown in hanging baskets or in pots having a 6-inch diameter and a depth of 8 inches.

In addition to the charm of their diminutive size, Miniature roses are known to be more disease-resistant than larger roses. 'Irresistible', like most other Miniatures, is surprizingly resilient throughout the winter. Most gardeners prune their Miniature roses as they would larger Hybrid Teas, and the amount of fertililzer is reduced a quarter.

(Polyantha), 'Tournament of Roses' (Grandiflora), and 'Irresistible' (Miniature) that she has received the coveted Best in Show award. Relying heavily on the recommendations of the American Rose Society's annual *Handbook for Selecting Roses* Ann-Mari never grows roses that have a rating of less than 7.3.

"I grow my roses for show and therefore the timing of the feeding is important," she claims. Fertilizing begins in April with monthly applications thereafter. If she knows the show date is the last week in September, she counts back six weeks, making sure that the roses are fed with either Mills Magic Rose Mix or Espoma's Rose Tone, both of which are organic fertilizers available through mail order. In addition to the regular monthly feeding, the roses in Ann-Mari's Virginia garden receive an annual sprinkling of bulk potassium early in the spring and two foliar feedings early in March and again in mid-August of Sea Riches from Gardens Alive, both of which she credits for the strikingly large blooms.

"Vigilance in the garden is the best protection," Ann-Mari claims. "A little maintenance every day lets me know my plants." She can observe at the earliest stages if insects or fungus are on the attack and can take action, which

often prevents more toxic and time-consuming spraying. At the first sign of damage from thrips, aphids, spider mites, or Japanese beetles (the nemesis for almost all rose gardeners), Ann-Mari tries the most ecologically safe remedies first: hand-picking the insect-damaged leaves or, later in the season, the tedious but effective hand-collecting of Japanese beetles; for aphids, who love the new, tender coppery leaves of early spring, she administers a thrice-weekly forceful spraying with water early in the morning on both the undersides and the tops of the infested leaves. Like many rosarians throughout the country, Ann-Mari balances her love of roses with a love of nature; she counts on the many birds she attracts to the garden to dispose of harmful insects. Good horticulture also keeps fungus diseases at bay.

Ann-Mari has learned from experience that if she gives her roses a moderate pruning in July, they will be usually ready for show by the end of September. Finally, even if there are summer showers, her soaking hoses are at work under the mulch for two hours every week. This aspect of rose culture helps to ensure the health of the show roses and to keep the garden disease free, which is perhaps the most important condition for perfect blooms. ❋

OPPOSITE Ann-Mari Horkan is known for the perfection of her prize-winning roses, including the 'Miss All American Beauty' shown here, a favorite since its introduction in 1965.

FOLLOWING PAGES, LEFT Roses have been so well integrated into the landscape that intriguing vistas abound at Claremont farm, such as through the boughs of luscious Golden Delicious apples in the nearby orchard. RIGHT Ann-Mari loves David Austin's 'Graham Thomas'.

"VIGILANCE IN THE GARDEN is the best protection," Ann-Mari claims. "A little maintenance every day lets me know my plants."

The GARDEN of TWO JUDGES

"IT STARTED IN 1984. I WAS ASKED TO BECOME THE ROSE CHAIRMAN FOR MY GARDEN CLUB, THE GARDEN CLUB OF THE NORTHERN NECK (A MEMBER CLUB OF THE GARDEN CLUB OF VIRGINIA). I KNEW NOTHING ABOUT GROWING ROSES AND VERY LITTLE ABOUT GARDENING. IN MY GARDEN

club, refusal to accept a job is frowned upon. So I began growing roses . . . just three bushes, only what we could comfortably handle." So Charlotte Hundley modestly explains the beginnings of the Hundley rose garden. She and her husband, Jim, have lived their entire lives in Virginia, mostly in their charmingly unpretentious 1795 house, Oakley (so named for the numerous century-old oaks that embellish the property), in the small town of Heathsville where they raised their children and enjoyed a life that included no roses until 1984. Today, their knowledge of and enthusiasm for roses has grown along with their garden. They "comfortably handle" 250 rose bushes, with more to be added as their interest in old garden roses continues to grow.

Along the way, Charlotte and Jim became consulting rosarians with the American Rose Society and later ARS horticulture judges, traveling around the country attending rose workshops and giving and attending lectures,

meetings, and rose shows that they either enter or judge, winning their own share of trophies and ribbons.

From the beginning, Charlotte knew the rose garden had to have at least 5 or 6 hours of sun, and the ideal spot for morning sun and for viewing from the family room was near the house. A 200-year-old maple makes an attractive backdrop for the rose garden, although its roots can often be deadly to the roses nearby.

When Jim retired in 1993 from his veterinary practice, he began to take as active an interest as his wife had in the world of roses. Both work in their garden together, but it is Jim whose scientific approach to gardening led him to redesign and enlarge the Hybrid Tea rose beds, based on easy access for maintenance.

When the Hundleys reminisce about their first design for a rose garden, Charlotte remembers that she wanted "an Oriental carpet look—not a garden of pinks and whites." Today,

their Hybrid Tea garden is much bigger (36 by 36 feet) than the original "Oriental carpet" garden and is even more vividly colorful because they like (and show) an ever-increasing number of roses of all colors.

As that garden grew into neat rows of prizewinning Hybrid Teas and Grandifloras (their favorites are 'Elina', 'Pristine', 'Jema', and 'Queen Elizabeth'), the Hundleys decided that a more relaxed bed with a variety of appropriate perennials was needed to show off their Floribundas and Miniature roses. Here, the ever-growing collection of Miniatures serves as a border, including the lovely pinkish apricot 'Jean Kenneally', which in 1993 was designated by the ARS evaluations as "the highest rated rose in America" [big or little] with a 9.7 (out of 10) rating. This rose has been reevaluated in the nine test roses gardens across the country and has continued to be the top-rated rose, both as a garden rose and for its exhibition quality.

RIGHT Beds of Hybrid Teas, Grandifloras, and Floribundas are the basis for Jim and Charlotte Hundley's prizewinning collection. From a screened porch, which the Hundleys added to their 18th-century house, friends and family can admire the garden.

BELOW 'Playboy' is one of the most popular Floribundas of all times. Its red blend classification is a misnomer, as its bright orange single petals tinged with yellow fairly glow in any garden. Both its single bloom and its prolific perfect sprays are often seen at rose show winners' tables.

PRECEDING PAGE The branches of a 200-year-old maple are as dramatic as the more than 200 spectacular roses beneath the tree at the Hundley rose garden on the Northern Neck Peninsula of Virginia.

OPPOSITE In 1911 the Danish breeder Dines Poulsen paved the way for the Floribunda family, while Eugene Boerner at Jackson & Perkins brought this modern class to new heights in the 1940s and established the Floribunda as the answer to a landscape designer's prayer: it is disease-resistant and hardy with a profusion of repeat blooms for an extended period. Shown here are three of the best: the orange standout 'Playboy', surrounded by 'Playgirl' on all sides, and pink 'Pleasure' in the foreground.

Among other highly rated roses (big and little), 'Irresistible', another Mini in the Hundley garden, was like 'Jean Kenneally' also hybridized by the late Dee Bennett and rates a 9.4. "It is an even better rose," according to Bennett's daughter, Sue O'Brien of Tiny Petals Nursery (see Sources), "because of its disease resistance and its ability to grow in more extreme climates." Another Miniature, rising fast on the ARS scale of exhibition Miniatures, is 'Fairhope', produced by Kay and Pete Taylor, owners of Taylor Roses—Miniatures Our Specialty (see Sources).

The person who is considered by all authorities to be "the King" of Miniature rose hybridizing is Ralph Moore of Visalia, California. Moore has devoted more than 60 years to this art and has produced many winners at the show table in the Rugosa and Floribunda classes as well as for his outstanding contribution to the field of Miniature roses, one of the most recent classes of Modern roses. Dating back to 1840, when the first Miniature rose was introduced in the United States, Miniature roses have continued to fascinate rose growers, both as exhibition specimens and as nonstop blooming showpieces in the garden. Ralph Moore's 'Magic Carousel', 'My Sunshine', and the 'Lavender Jewel' rank among the Miniature favorites throughout the country.

A very beautiful new Ralph Moore Floribunda—verging on a Miniature—is 'Blastoff'. It is also a new favorite prizewinner in the Hundley garden and, introduced in 1995, does not yet have an ARS rating. Although classified as a Floribunda, it grows no bigger than many of the Miniatures in the Hundley garden. Charlotte advises that when selecting Miniatures you should pay attention to the height. While the blossoms, foliage, and thorns of Miniature roses may be small, the plants often grow as large as a small Shrub rose.

Since the 19th century, when rosarians first began growing roses solely for competition, exhibitors' gardens have taken on an almost clinical look, as the owners focus on their prizewinning blooms rather than on the garden as a whole. Although Charlotte and Jim Hundley "grow for show," their rose garden is intended to give pleasure and to encourage all visitors to share in their love of the rose. ❊

BLASTOFF

Floribunda

This fiery little orange-blend Floribunda is often classified as a Miniature because one of its parent was the prizewinning 'Little Artist'. Developed by the "King of Miniatures" Ralph Moore in 1995, 'Blastoff' resembles the old Floribundas in that it has multiple smaller flowers clustering on very large sprays. Yet its medium-size blossoms grown in large clusters are thoroughly modern because of their eye-popping colors of reddish-orange and scarlet with a contrasting white reverse. The name 'Blastoff' is apt, suggesting the explosion of color it makes in the garden. Its ruffled bicolored petals are numerous (35 to 40) and full of substance, making 'Blastoff' as long lasting in the garden as it is in a floral arrangement.

The Hundleys grow the small, upright, yet larger-than-Miniature bush in the back of their Miniature bed where it is in perfect scale. Its deep glossy green leaves set off the bright fully double blooms, making it a good addition to any perennial border even when not in bloom. The extremely long-lived blossoms of 'Blastoff' can last over a week on the bush.

In addition to its decorative attributes, excellent disease resistance and ease of growing make 'Blastoff' another success for its introducer, Weeks Roses. At the show table as a Floribunda spray, 'Blastoff' has proven to be a winner, both for the Hundleys in Virginia and for others throughout the country.

OPPOSITE Prizewinning Miniature roses have a special charm meriting a place of their own in the Hundley garden. Masses of them shown here are the tallest, 'Jean Kenneally', an apricot-blend; the deep coral-pink 'Millie Walters'; on the right, a pink blend, 'Giggles'; and behind, the white 'Irresistible'. Charlotte Hundley has mixed in a few perennials to complement the Minis: Veronica, Snapdragons, Yarrow, Phlox, Caryopteris, and Daylilies.

A TOUCH *of* SOUTHERN CHARM

THERE IS SOMETHING QUINTESSENTIALLY SOUTHERN ABOUT MARY HART ORR'S ROSE GAR-
DEN. SEPARATED FROM THE REST OF THE 1-ACRE GARDEN SHE SHARES WITH HER HUSBAND,
DON, IN GREENSBORO, NORTH CAROLINA, MARY HART'S PRIVATE SANCTUARY IS FRAMED BY

roses and outlined by native hemlocks, pin oaks (*Quercus palustris*), and styrax, with its aura of quiet charm. The colors—pinks, whites, and pale blues—underline the feeling of softness, and even the elusive scent seems unique to the South; in the late spring are intermingling magnolias, roses, mock orange, and snowbell blossoms. Yet, as Mary Hart Orr's daughter, Mary Michaels, put it, "What I love about this garden is perhaps also true of southern women. Under the veneer of softness there is an amazing strength. This garden, under its prettiness, is about thorns and strength and structure."

The oval-centered rose garden in the back yard of the property began in 1981, with the death of one of the area's last Dutch elms (*Ulmus hollandica*). Another large tree, one of the magnolias that required daily cleanup of large leaves from the ground, was removed at the same time. Suddenly, instead of an immense obstruction, hours of mainte-

nance, and an abundance of shade, there was space and light. "When I returned home from school one day as a ten-year-old to find the upturned dirt and nothingness, it was horrifying," Mary Michels admits, "but to my mother it was the beginning of rebirth."

The "rebirth" involved taking down the fence, eradicating the Bermuda grass, and adding truckloads of soil conditioner and topsoil to change the grade and fill in the swamp behind the house, which formerly dropped 6 feet outside the back door. An additional obstacle, the bamboolike forest, innocently planted as a screen by Mary Hart's parents-in-law fifteen years earlier, had almost taken over the entire space and required three years to remove completely. Stage 1 had begun. New irrigation was put in and Mary Hart, her helper, William Graves, and his son, William Jr., were then ready for building a new garden—where roses were the bones, not the ornaments.

They used strings and grids to get the perfect oval within the rectangular area that was already there. "I knew in my mind what I wanted: a dead center which would be on the axis down through the gate and arbor to the side yard." The arbor had been put in that particular spot because it was in the middle of the newly created bank. The view, from the outside of the garden across a lush green lawn to the rose-covered arbor, invites visitors to enter a magical place.

The first of a collection of roses in Mary Hart's garden had been the seven 'America' Large-flowered Climbers. These vigorous growers, when later moved out of the enclosed lattice fenced area, gave more space inside the newly created rose garden. The large salmon-pink blooms of the 'Climbing Americas', dating back to 1981, define the outer limits of the garden along the fence and commingle over the arched gateway with 'New Dawn', another

RHONDA

Large-flowered Climber

One of the climbing roses most consistently found in American gardens is the first patented rose (1930) 'New Dawn'. Less well known is 'Rhonda', one of its numerous offspring produced by the American breeder Lissemore and introduced by Conard-Pyle in 1968. Having many of the same characteristics as its parent, 'Rhonda' was celebrated for 20 years after its introduction as a vigorous 10-foot grower, repeat-bloomer, and a long-lasting Large-flowered Climber (LCL), before it fell into relative obscurity.

In her garden, Mary Hart Orr uses 'Rhonda' and other Large-flowered Climbers strategically, taking advantage of the opulence of their blooms, which add to the screening, climb over an entrance gate, and lightly swing into garlands of color. Typical of this thoroughly modern class, 'Rhonda' has many uses in the garden. Its large carmine-pink, mildly fragrant double blooms decorate many a pillar, pergola, and wall. Mary Hart Orr has imaginatively defined the limits of her Greensboro, North Carolina, garden with swags of 'Rhonda' that repeat and repeat their medium-pink blooms. Between bloom cycles the glossy, disease-resistant foliage tied along graceful supports maintains a pleasing architectural shape.

When trained to curve along a support or horizontally against a wall, the long, rather flexible canes of LCLs produce many lateral shoots which should be pruned annually to 2 or 3 inches for the next season's blooms.

Large-flowered Climber introduced in 1930 that became suddenly popular in the 1950s and continues to be a favorite with many American gardeners today.

"At first I didn't want to add anything but 'Pristine'. I loved the size of the canes, the deepness of the green leaves, and its long, pointed buds that open to the softest pink imaginable." It was the rose of choice to outline the oval, but it turned out they were not ever-blooming enough. So the outline became 'Bonica' shrubs. Mary Hart explained, "I loved its color and how bountifully it blooms. It lends itself to almost any color put beside it." Blue scabiosa and *Corydalis cashmeriana* 'Blue Panda' lightened by baby's breath (*Gypsophila paniculata*) are particularly effective when grown next to the clusters of 'Bonica' roses.

During Stage 2, Mary Hart introduced punctuations of two standard pink tree roses—'The Fairy' and 'China Doll'—along the oval outline. She put these in terra-cotta pots with under-plantings of variegated ivy, rosemary, Swan River daisies (*Brachycome iberidifolia*), and trailing white zinnias. "It still needed more height and was so very flat. That was when I got the wrought-iron man to put up some vertical pillars." At this point, another beautiful rose came into the garden to enhance the picture Mary Hart had in her mind—'Rhonda', a third and somewhat forgotten Large-flowered Climber, a seedling of 'New Dawn', whose canes climb the wrought-iron poles (originally designed to support bird-feeding stations) and whose carmine blooms abundantly cover the garlands of iron bands. "The garlands were so much better than a fence-enclosed garden because they do add a feeling of airiness and yet they provided the final touch of privacy." This was an absolute necessity for its owner, who loves her garden, above all, as a peace-restoring place where she can "sit, pull the chickweed, and get centered again." ❈

OPPOSITE The entrance to this garden is marked by two terra-cotta pots of Polyanthas trained as standards: 'Climbing China Doll' and 'The Fairy', both subtle shades of pink that complement the carmine-rose double blooms of 'Rhonda' on the metal garlands above. Underplanting the pots and filling the beds nearby, a variety of annuals and perennials abound, including variegated ivy and trailing white zinnias, Swan River daisies, pink verbena and dianthus, gypsophila, and blue campanulas.

PRECEDING PAGE Few climbers can surpass the pale pink 'New Dawn' for its hardiness, disease resistance, and profusion of blooms throughout the season. Its companion on the far side of the arbor is another Large-flowered Climber, 'America', introduced in 1976 by the great hybridizer William Warriner of Jackson & Perkins.

OLD ROSES *at the* PLANTATION

THE BONES OF THE 1930S BUTTERFLY-SHAPED GARDEN WERE STILL IN EVIDENCE IN 1995 AT BOONE HALL PLANTATION, LOCATED SIX MILES NORTH OF CHARLESTON, SOUTH CAROLINA, WHEN RUTH KNOPF WAS CALLED IN AS GARDEN CONSULTANT. NO DOCUMENTATION EXISTED

for the planting scheme, however, and the present owner of the plantation, William H. McRae, had no preconceived ideas about it. Ruth's reputation as a garden designer and knowledgeable rosarian, as well as a collector of old roses, particularly of Noisettes and Teas, is renown. Over the years her own collection has enriched those of rose growers across the country. Ruth was given carte blanche to devise a plan. She retained the formal butterfly design and embellished it with an informal planting scheme that was at once unique, beautiful, and historically intriguing.

The twenty-four beds were harmoniously connected by the wonderful old roses that perform so well in the South: Chinas, Noisettes, and Teas. Ruth started the planting with her favorite rose class, four beds of typically fragrant Teas, including 'Mrs. B. R. Cant', 'Safrano', and 'Baronne Henriette de Snoy'. The mirrored symmetry on either side of the wide axial path was accentuated by a later addition of

fourteen pillars covered with climbing varieties of Noisettes, Teas, Hybrid Musks, and even a favorite climbing China, the red 'Cramoisi Superieur'. Some of the most successful used as pillars are Tea-Noisettes: the soft yellow-blossomed 'Lamarque' that fades to white and 'Crépuscule' with a double-flowered orange bloom that fades to a rich apricot-yellow. Ruth has arranged her symmetrical planting scheme carefully so that soft yellow, apricot, and gold balance each other on both sides of the path nearest the entrance while the pinks, whites, and mauves of the Teas fade into each other in the matching beds that fan out in front of the mansion.

Although Boone Hall was rebuilt in the 1930s, its land grant dates to 1681. There is no documentation for the original house, but Ruth Knopf believed the garden should reflect the feeling of gardens before the modern rose era, when roses grew naturally and freely, without pruning or pampering,

among other favorite garden plants of the owner's choice. As the Boone Hall Plantation garden matures, Ruth continues to draw on her superb knowledge of plants in finding those companions that are not only rose enhancing and color harmonizing but also ones that might have been used by 18th- and 19th-century South Carolina gardeners.

The class of China roses is particularly well represented at Boone Hall. In addition to their ongoing blooms and historic appropriateness, Ruth Knopf chose Chinas for Boone Hall because of their hardiness and, finally, for their beauty as shrubs in the garden even when not in bloom. Their light, airy foliage creates a soft, informal feeling; the blooms bow on tender stems with their weight and offer a perfume— often tea scented—that makes a stroll in the evening hours an unforgettable experience.

Boone Hall has excellent examples of the unusual China 'Green Rose', *Rosa*

RIGHT The orange-apricot Tea-Noisette 'William Allen Richardson' stands out in its delicacy amid strong orange and yellow cannas, French marigolds, and coreopsis.

BELOW Ruth Knopf stands next to one of her favorites, 'Perle d'Or', an early Polyantha that was crossed with a Tea rose to produce an old-fashioned look. The rose garden at Boone Hall is unique, because the garden displays roses as they were grown in the last century, with annuals and perennials in the same beds.

PRECEDING PAGE A "found" rose from Bermuda, 'Miss Atwood' is a very fragrant apricot-blush Tea rose. Boone Hall in the background was completely rebuilt in 1930.

chinensis viridiflora, which mounds up in a green shrubby profusion of blooms that are not really blooms at all but sepals that look like blossoms and are a flower arranger's delight in bronze and green. 'Mutabilis' (*R. chinensis mutabilis*), another China, perhaps the best known throughout the country, begins with orange buds that open to a sulphur yellow and change to pink, orange, and a darker crimson all on the bush at the same time.

In addition to the Chinas, Teas, and Noisettes, Ruth has planted some modern roses that also do well in southern climes, such as Hybrid Musks and Polyanthas. Their loose, often clustered blooms in pale colors lend an authentic note to the Boone Hall Plantation. "We don't exclude plants that are *not* old, but if they have an old look, we use them," Ruth explained.

Ruth's garden philosophy is to let the beauty of nature come through: "You can't improve upon nature. Roses are more beautiful grown naturally. When you whack at them they can't grow the way they are supposed to." The same is true for spraying. "Old roses were never sprayed before chemicals came to be used with modern roses, so I spray only when thrips are present or there is a persistent disease problem. Usually if we spray two weeks in a row, that takes care of it. I also don't like chemical fertilizers and use mostly chicken and cow manure and lots of compost. Ruth says that by avoiding high-nitrogen fertilizers the plants are encouraged to grow stronger in a natural way and "they won't have so much sappy growth, and this also helps reduce the insect and disease problem." The practice of pegging roses (arching the canes and then pegging or tying down the ends) is popular among rosarians who want the maximum amount of bloom. Teas and Chinas, with their upright growth habit, are considered by some to be ideal for pegging, but Ruth's philosophy of letting the plant grow naturally does not require pegging at Boone Hall. "I think of roses as plants grown for their garden value, not just for their blooms alone."

The privately owned plantation is open to visitors throughout the year, but for rose lovers who want to see one of America's most beautiful collection of Chinas, Teas, and Noisettes, the best, most dependable time to visit is in the fall, when the roses are offering their most impressive show. ❆

GREEN ROSE

China

Although 'Green Rose' (*Rosa chinensis viridiflora*) is an unusual member of the China rose class, it shares some of the growth habits with other China roses. It was exported from China much earlier than it was first marketed in the United States, in 1856. At that time it was described by the Philadelphia nurseryman Robert Buist as having come from Charleston from a sport of the *R. indica*, the English China rose. Its medium upright growth is typical of other China roses. However, its greenish blooms, which are actually sepals, are not typical of the class, but rather demonstrate its versitility.

Nineteenth-century rosarians did not particularly appreciate *R. chinensis viridiflora*, but were intrigued by its oddity and hardiness when compared to other Chinas. Today, however, its long-blooming bronzy flowers have inspired many floral arrangers. Its pointed buds are exactly the same color as its pointed leaves, making them hard to spot in the garden from a distance. When close at hand, though, one marvels at the light green freshness of its fully opened buds. Around Christmastime in warmer climates some of its petals turn a decorative bronze.

Other popular and more typical Chinas with nodding, lightly scented blooms are 'Old Blush', 'Hermosa', and 'Cramoisie Superieur', all of which have a free-flowing habit in the garden.

KNOPF BELIEVED the garden should reflect
the feeling of gardens before the modern rose
era, when roses grew naturally....

NOTHING COULD BE FINER

IF YOU HAVE EVER WALKED ALONG THE STREETS OF CHARLESTON IN MAY, YOU HAVE NO DOUBT SEEN TRUSSES OF ROSES WITH THEIR CASCADING CLUSTERS OF SOFTLY COLORED BLOSSOMS DRAPED OVER WROUGHT-IRON GATES, OR CLINGING TO PICKET FENCES AND BRICK

walls, or standing as pillars of splendor in back yards. And you have no doubt had an intoxicating whiff of their clove- or tea-scented fragrance. The rose is the pride of South Carolina's finest: the Noisette.

If 'Champneys' Pink Cluster' is Charleston's most typical rose, then the Noisette is the class par excellence for the entire state, for nowhere else does the Noisette grow better than in the hot, humid southern climate where the first Noisette was born. And nowhere do Noisettes (and Chinas, Teas, and hundreds of other roses, for that matter) seem happier than in the garden of Pat Henry, co-owner of Roses Unlimited, a nursery not far from her nine-acre wooded property in northwestern South Carolina. Pat enjoys propagating roses. She grows them on their own rootstock from cuttings and has over the years success- fully added two new named Flori- bunda roses to the long list of patented

roses in America: 'Charlotte Ann' and 'Katelyn Ann'; the latter one was named for her granddaughter.

One of the rose growers Pat admires most is the late Griffith Buck from Iowa, one of America's greatest hy- bridizers. Buck is best known for 'Carefree Beauty', one of the most pop- ular roses throughout the country since its introduction in 1978. Loved both for its charm in the garden and for its almost total disease resistance, 'Carefree Beauty' is but one of Buck's successful introductions. His roses, although usu- ally associated with the midwest and northern zones (3–6)—where they are much appreciated for their winter hardi- ness—have been adopted by gardeners in warmer climates, too. In Pat Henry's Zone 7 garden, she loves growing many Buck roses—including 'Carefree Beauty', 'Country Dancer', and 'Distant Drums'—just for the beauty of their large rose-pink and lavender double blooms, but she has to admit that their

almost carefree maintenance is an added plus, making them a joy in any garden.

When the Henrys built their house in 1981, they took advantage of the beautiful wooded area of native birch, pine, hickory, sweet gum, maple, and oak that was on the property and that today borders her Wooded Garden. In fall, the leaves of burnt umber, gold, and burgundy tumble into a carpet mixed with rose petals. The roots of the trees are not a threat, for she has planted more than 200 of her 600 roses in containers, which enables her to test the roses in a specific area in their 1-gallon pots until she knows exactly where they will look best in the garden. Another advantage is that the effects of water and fertilizer are con- centrated at the roots, even when the containers are buried in the ground.

Pat Henry carefully monitors her ongoing testing of the shade tolerance of roses. Many of her experiments dis- prove the age-old rule that roses must

have 6 hours of sun. In Pat's garden, many of the Musks, Teas, and Chinas are in partial shade and receive only 4½ hours of sunshine each day. Through the years, Pat has found that 'Penelope' (Hybrid Musk), 'Charlotte Ann' (Floribunda), and 'Champneys' Pink Cluster' (Noisette) thrive in partial shade if they have good air circulation to avoid fungus problems. When grown in their 1-gallon containers, she can acclimatize by moving them deeper and deeper into the woods each year.

Pat Henry, like many American rosarians across the country, claims that her roses are successful in part because of the fertilizer she uses: Mills Magic Rose Mix, a completely organic blend prepared by Beaty Fertilizer in Cleveland, Tennessee. "It has everything a rose needs and it is so easy to use. I just scratch it into my one-gallon containers with a kitchen fork and the results are amazing!"

Asked to choose a favorite in her garden, Pat has trouble selecting among the fragrant Noisettes she offers through her mail-order catalog—particularly the pale yellows like 'Alister Stella Gray' and 'Celine Forestier' or the exquisite old French 'Lamarque', whose lemon clusters reach into her dogwood tree and light up the wooded garden. But most likely, if she had to choose only one rose for every day, it would be the buds of the vigorous, hardy, and continuously fragrant 'Blush Noisette', the original offspring of 'Champneys' Pink Cluster', because they link both her and her relatively new garden with South Carolina's past. ❊

BLUSH NOISETTE

Noisette

'Blush Noisette' was reputedly the first offspring of 'Champney's Pink Cluster', whose origins predate 1817. 'Blush Noisette', in Pat Henry's garden, is particularly rewarding when the hot days of summer leave most other roses withering. Even after weeks of over 90° F. weather, 'Blush Noisette' will produce its pale pink blossoms that fade to a silky white, creating a stunning contrast to the darker pink buds that continue to reappear throughout the fall.

In most gardens, 'Blush Noisette' forms a short, bushy, upright shrub with a profusion of fragrant blooms. These blooms grow in clusters at the ends of numerous smooth canes reaching up to 8 feet in height and 6 feet across. As Graham Stuart Thomas observed, 'Blush Noisette' is often seen "peeping over a garden wall, or sometimes it is grown up a house wall to 15 feet." Often it appears as a medium hedge, particularly in the South. In all cases the clove scent of this continuous bloomer permeates the garden. In colder areas, protection is needed or at least a warm wall for this delicate beauty to cling to. Noisettes are usually considered more tender than their Southern sister classes, the Chinas and Teas, and less resistant to blackspot and mildew.

OPPOSITE 'Monsieur Tillier' grows successfully in the South and has become a favorite Tea rose choice because of its very fragrant flowers and the unique coloration of its blooms. Echoing the fall colors, its quartered flowers are remarkable: a brick color with hints of salmon and a warm pink glow.

PRECEDING PAGE Fall is often the best time for roses in the Carolinas as the leaves turn golden amber. Here, streaks of sunshine highlight 'Rhonda' on the arch made by Pat's husband Rex of home-grown cedar saplings and muscadine vine.

THREE

AT *the* CENTER *of the* COUNTRY

In the Mississippi Valley, the Gulf Coast, and Texas, conditions vary so greatly that from the standpoint of climate and soil, no general rule for the culture of roses holds. In the summer, high humidity and heat prevail from subtropical New Orleans to temperate St. Louis. In the winter, in some parts of Texas and the Midwest, temperatures dip to subzero. Neither extreme is ideal for growing roses! And yet, ingenious mid-country gardeners have created some of the most beautiful rose gardens in the nation, carefully selecting suitable varieties, fertilizing, watering, pruning, and winterizing their plants when necessary. ❈ The gardens here reflect different traditions, all maintained in lively and creative fashion by their owners. In Louisiana, the Holdens designed their garden *à la française* and utilized old garden roses as well as indigenous plants the early French immigrants would have used in their Creole gardens. ❈ In Texas, the "Rose Rustlers" have influenced a new generation of rosarians, whose gardening activities have made them into explorers. Caravaning along the backroads since the early 1980s, they have discovered lost or forgotten rose varieties left to grow wild in old graveyards and along the verandas of abandoned homesteads.

Founding Rustler Mike Shoup, is today the owner of the Antique Rose Emporium, a nursery begun with stock from the early finds, and artist David Caton has had a long love affair with Texas natives, which he has mixed in his small suburban garden with those roses that are aesthetically compatible and which were to be found in abandoned towns and cemeteries of the last century. Texas has a more formal side as well: the English gardening tradition was reintroduced in Fort Worth by the distinguished landscape architect Russell Page, when he was asked to design a rose garden befitting Anne Bass's elegant Texas home. Here, the rose garden is a distinct entity, separate from the rest of the garden, and the roses are predominantly Hybrid Teas and Polyanthas of the hardiest kind. The Kroegers' garden in St. Louis, also in the English tradition, sits in a parklike setting of large trees. Finally, the profiled roses in this important geographic section emphasize the importance of the burgeoning modern rose classes in the ongoing history of the rose after 1867.

OPPOSITE POPPIES AND LARKSPUR WITH 'LOUIS PHILIPPE' AT MAISON CHENAL.
PRECEDING PAGE THORNS FROM AN OLD ORANGE TREE AND 'FISHERMAN'S FRIEND' IN DAVID CATON'S GARDEN.

A REMEMBRANCE *of* THINGS PAST

THROUGH INTELLIGENT RESEARCH AND CAREFUL COLLECTING, DR. JACK HOLDEN AND HIS WIFE, PATSY, HAVE CREATED A SLICE OF 18TH- AND EARLY-19TH-CENTURY CREOLE LIFE ON THEIR 75-ACRE PROPERTY AT MAISON CHENAL. THEIR AUTHENTICALLY RESTORED HOUSE IS ON

the Bayou Chenal, one of Louisiana's narrow channel-like tributaries of the Mississippi River. Before 1722, Chenal was the main bayou. While there are touches of English, early American, German, and African in Creole, Patsy says that the Creole style "is mostly an intriguing juxtaposition of a sophisticated French flair with the Louisiana frontier reality."

In 1975, shortly after purchasing their property with the bayou running through it, the Holdens found an authentic late-18th-century Creole plantation house that they were able to move from 11 miles away. Over the next twenty years, they also moved several dependencies of the early 19th century onto the property and had them restored: a *pigeonnier,* which is still used as a dovecote; a kitchen house; a *garçonnière,* and a former overseer's quarters today exquisitely appointed with period Louisiana antiques and used as a guest house. The Holdens permit only the most authentic restoration, which adds

to the nostalgic atmosphere and heightens a sense of old Louisiana.

At Maison Chenal, the front garden is based on a design of two central lozenges, set off by axial walkways covered in pea gravel, as were the traditional gardens of France. In addition, each of the squares is sectioned off by the Creole equivalent of boxwood—a necessity in any traditional French garden—that is feral privet, *Ligustrum sinense.* Geometric patterned beds are punctuated by several antique roses, native yaupon (*Ilex vomitoria*), a sago palm (*Cycas revoluta*), and a specimen pineapple plant. The basic garden plan continues the same informal yet stylized *à la française* feeling the Holdens have recreated indoors with objects in their "material culture collection": paintings, sketches, bibelots, furniture, kitchenware, and china.

The rectangular garden behind the house is based on an 18th-century sketch by Dumont de Montigny of his own garden near New Orleans. In addi-

tion to unpublished documents, letters, and parish records, the Holdens relied heavily on *Le Nouveau Jardinier de la Louisiane,* published in Louisiana in 1838, for their lists of vegetables, herbs, and flowers. The Holdens felt it appropriate to keep a parterred garden arrangement that could be looked down upon from the second-story gallery surrounding the house. Their goal was, like that of the French who came before them, to intermix a less formal group of Louisiana native plants such as sago palms, ferns from the swamps, the native flowering rudbeckia, coreopsis, wild ageratum, spiderwort, and cleomes with some of the volunteering plants, such as tufts of balsam (*Impatiens balsamina*) and penstemon that appear randomly in the otherwise well-structured planting scheme. Along with these natives the Holdens have interspersed a small collection of exotics (larkspur, jasmines, poppies, and roses), which their research told them were used in early Creole gardens. The more relaxed Old World

ABOVE The lozenge shape, based on early 19th century notarial archive drawings, a favorite of Creole cabinet makers, is used prominently in the Maison Chenal patterned garden.

RIGHT Repeat-blooming China roses, such as 'Old Blush', were a familiar sight in Europe after their introduction into England prior to 1759. Creole gardeners of the late 18th and 19th centuries found them easy to grow in their "à la française" Louisiana gardens.

PRECEDING PAGE A beautiful still life features flowers available to the early French settlers in Louisiana: penstemon, larkspur, trumpet honeysuckle, and roses, in an early 19th-century Vieux Paris porcelain vase.

FOLLOWING PAGES Patsy and Jack Holden insist on authenticity in their collection of Creole objets d'art and in their garden as well. Here the lichen-covered cypress picket *"pieux"* fence surrounds the geometric privet parterres, a Creole adaptation of the classic French garden.

plants such as rose geranium (*Pelargonium graveoleus*), Trumpet honeysuckle (*Lonicera sempervirens*), and large-leafed mulleins along with native lantana create a softening effect as they tumble outside their orderly French lines.

In the first quarter of the 19th century in Louisiana, the newly arrived French ladies and their Creole neighbors struggled touchingly to maintain gardens that would follow French traditions but would thrive in the new climate and place. Along with hope for a better life, many of the early French settlers brought with them a well-articulated garden style that included roses, the latest fashion in France.

French roses are at the base of the Holden exotica collection, in particular Chinas, Teas, Noisettes, and Bourbons, which were enthusiastically sought after in colonial Louisiana just as they were in France immediately after their introduction in the late 18th and early 19th centuries. The lichen-covered cypress picket fence at the Holden garden is referred to locally as a *pieux* fence and is attractively decorated with the 'Old Blush' China and Tea roses: the highly fragrant 'Duchesse de Brabant' and 'Louis Philippe'. Other members of these same old rose families are scattered throughout the garden, lending a historical note as well as their fragrance and graceful form. Offering a particular charm not restricted to France are 'Sombreuil', a favorite Tea rose in many American gardens today, and another southern favorite offered by the Antique Rose Emporium called 'Natchitoches

Noisette', which identifies the rose with its "found" location at an 18th-century fort in nearby Natchitoches. Both respond luxuriantly in the Holden garden to the abundant rainfall and subtropical climate of Louisiana and give the garden a certain lushness characteristic of Creole gardens in general.

Fragrance pervades the Holden garden, all from plants mentioned as companions in *Le Nouveau Jardinier:* sweet olive (*Osmanthus fragrans*), honeysuckle, several jasmines including the 'Arabian' variety (*Jasminum sambac*), "Carolina jasmine" (*Gelsemium sempervirens*), the "night-blooming" jasmine (*Cestrum nocturnum*), and "Cape jasmine" (*Gardenia jasminoides* 'Fortuniana'). The roses the Holdens selected are typical of those grown in most reconstructed Creole gardens today. They suggest the strong connection with the mother country and are roses that were very popular in France in the 18th and 19th centuries.

In the 1970s, the Holdens received cuttings of old roses, such as 'Clotilde Soupert' and 'Duchesse de Brabant', from the late Ruth Robinson Fontenot, whom Jack describes as a sorely missed "*bonne* Creole." Fontenot's own garden roses started as cuttings from a garden that had once belonged to Gabriel Pierre Wartelle, one of Napoleon's soldiers. The Holdens continue to pass along cuttings to friends who admire the roses at Maison Chenal and who want to keep in touch with Louisiana's fragrant horticultural past. ❈

DUCHESSE DE BRABANT

Tea

Sean McCann, the distinguished Irish rosarian, wrote about 'Duchesse de Brabant': "When you see a full, rampant bush of say 'Duchesse de Brabant' big, full, loose, fragrant blooms, then you will know what beauty is all about." Teddy Roosevelt showed his appreciation of this old-fashioned favorite by wearing it so often as a boutonniere that it became one of his signatures. The fully cupped, warm pink rose has remained popular since its introduction in 1857, and the normally 4- to 6-foot attractive bush is often found in old gardens and cemeteries. It flowers repeatedly, is one of the hardiest of the Teas, and its fragrant blooms make it one of the most popular Old Garden Roses even where globular roses tend not to open because of the humidity.

It was named after the Hungarian-born Marie Henriette, the Duchess of Brabant and later Queen of Belgium for 37 years, who endured a loveless marriage for 49 years to the unfaithful Leopold. A French hybridizer in Marseilles, H. B. Bernede, is given credit for producing the rose, which in Europe was called 'Comtesse de LaBarthe'. In America, 19th-century nurserymen offered the same rose as 'Duchesse de Brabant'. Whoever named it, many have felt that the graceful nodding blossoms suggested a note of sadness commensurate with the life of its namesake.

ALONG WITH HOPE for a better life, many of the early French settlers brought with them a well-articulated garden style that included roses, the latest fashion in France.

ROSE RUSTLING

OFFICIALLY, DAVID CATON IS AN ARTIST, BUT HE IS ALSO ONE OF TEXAS'S MOST ARDENT "ROSE RUSTLERS," THE BAND OF ADVENTUROUS SOULS WHO EXPLORE TEXAS BACKROADS IN SEARCH OF LOST OR FORGOTTEN ROSES. ORIGINALLY, DAVID HAD DEVOTED THE 34 BY 64-FOOT BACK

yard of his modest suburban home to a collection of Texas natives, but his desire to find other beautiful subjects for his paintings and a serendipitous encounter with the Rustlers prompted him to redesign his property with an interesting blend of plants and bold design elements.

David's front garden stands out because he has made no attempt to imitate the standard suburban landscape of a lawn and foundation plantings. Instead, he has juxtaposed boulders, flagstones, native Texas grasses, succulents, and ground-covering herbs with a collection of native-grown roses inspired by his association with the Texas Rose Rustlers.

The history of rose rustling is short and very recent. In the early 1980s, Pam Puryear, the unofficial head of the group, and a handful of other Rustlers caravanned along Texas backroads, visiting old graveyards and abandoned homesteads in search of lost or forgotten roses that had grown wild. The old

roses' survival against the odds of heat, drought, humidity, and neglect ensured that they were ideal for their environment. Later, Mike Shoup, owner of the Antique Rose Emporium, and Dr. William C. Welch, a highly regarded landscape horticulturist and professor at Texas A&M, who had done some rustling in Louisiana and the Carolinas, joined in with their knowledge and enthusiasm. In some cases, Rustlers have actually succeeded in saving roses in danger of extinction.

A relative newcomer to the rose rustling group, David expressed characteristic enthusiasm in remembering an early encounter with the group: "I'll never forget the excitement of that rustle with Marion and Frances Brandes in the early 1990s in San Felipe, Texas, when we found a Noisette none of us had ever seen." The cutting produced in David's garden a climber whose pale yellow blooms offer a fragrant reminder of that early rustle, but the "foundling" still remains unnamed. Today, David

points with pleasure and pride to another "found" rose that came from the same rustle in the small rural town of Wallace, Texas. David brought home his cuttings, and though he didn't know their names at first, they did "still smell as sweet" (just as Shakespeare said they would) when one was later identified as the Tea rose 'Marie Van Houtte'. Even when the cupped yellow and pink-tinged blossoms are not in bloom, the glossy dark shrub is still an appealing plant for an artist's garden.

"I probably have seventy-five to eighty roses today, but my first love was the Texas natives. As that collection kept growing and as I became more successful at growing roses from cuttings, I found they looked well together and this combination became the focus of my garden design."

David's favorite Chinas—'Ducher', 'Louis Philippe', and 'Mutabilis'—although not native to Texas, grow so luxuriantly and easily that they might as well be indigenous. Teas, like Chinas,

are heat loving and have become the next most popular class among Texas old rose growers. Those in David's garden add enormously to his colorful palette and well-constructed design. 'Sombreuil', which is perhaps the best known of all the Tea roses, climbs 12 feet up the trellis in his patio garden, offering its delicious Tea fragrance even on the warmest Houston summer evening. Sharing the trellis with 'Sombreuil' is 'Maggie', a found rose from Louisiana that Dr. Welch named for his grandmother and that the Antique Rose Emporium now sells all over the South because of its beautiful fragrant, carmine blooms, and easy growth habit.

In addition to the Chinas, Teas, and a few Noisettes, David has put at the back of his garden several David Austin English roses, some of which, like 'Fisherman's Friend', he allows to grow as tall and sprawling as they want. He keeps the height of others in check by radical pruning. In addition, withholding water to some degree seems to help control the growth.

Among the most prized blooms in David Caton's rose collection are his Polyanthas—a class of low-growing showstoppers—grouped among the rocks with lime green sedums, artemisia, and the native ground cover *Stemodia tomentosa* nearby. The cream-colored native limestone boulders offer a strong structural contrast to the deep green foliage of 'Clotilde Soupert'. The name of this pale pink beauty with an old-fashioned look is a reminder of the French origins of its relatively modern class. 'Mrs. R. M. Finch', an especially hardy Polyantha, invariably catches the eye of passersby, with its delicate clusters of bright rosy-pink and large-flowered blooms. This almost ever-blooming Polyantha enjoys a special place right in the front of David Caton's yard, where there is almost always something in flower—usually a rose. ❋

CLOTILDE SOUPERT

Polyanthas

'Clotilde Soupert', along with its more famous sister, 'Cecile Brunner', belongs to the modern class of roses that was introduced in the 1890s called Polyanthas, or Poly-Pompons. When the rambling Multiflora rose was first bred with a pink China in France, the result was a new class of roses that produced repeat-blooming, multiclustering small flowers on a compact, low-growing bush.

The very fragrant blooms of 'Clotilde Soupert' are not as small as those of its ancestors 'Mignonette' and 'Paquerette', produced by Guillot a decade earlier, but its 100 petals unfurl into a round cabbage-shaped rose with a rich rose-pink center fading out to creamy white. The profusion of its repeat-flowering blooms on a small shrub (3 to 4 feet) of light green leaves made it a favorite among the Victorians, and today it is a landscape designer's treasure. It can be grown as an outstanding speciman plant or as a hedge that is rarely out of bloom.

Polyanthas are hardy to Zone 5, and 'Clotilde Soupert' grows as well in David Caton's garden in Houston as it does in the Holdens' Louisiana garden. This disputes the criticism that small Polyanthas do not always open properly under humid conditions. When sheared after each bloom cycle, they can be kept neat and compact and will add greatly to the perennial bed.

OPPOSITE On the Houston artist's patio, vigorous branches of the carmine red 'Maggie' are gracefully entwined with a white 'Sombreuil', the best known of the old-fashioned climbing Teas. The Texas horticulturist Dr. William C. Welch of Texas A&M University first collected and propagated this beautiful red rose he named 'Maggie', which is now available through the Antique Rose Emporium.

PRECEDING PAGE Roses, including 'Highway 290 Pink Buttons', which was found on an outing with the Texas Rose Rustlers, are juxtaposed behind a section of David Caton's collection of boulders, flagstones, native Texas grasses, and succulents.

LONE STAR ELEGANCE

ONE OF THE LAST PRIVATE GARDENS RUSSELL PAGE CREATED BEFORE HIS DEATH IN 1985 WAS AT THE STARKLY MODERN HOUSE DESIGNED BY PAUL RUDOLPH IN FORT WORTH, TEXAS, FOR ART PATRON AND PHILANTHROPIST ANNE H. BASS. IN 1976, CONSTRUCTION HAD BEEN COMPLETED

and landscape architect Robert Zion had finished the serenely beautiful landscaping around the estate. At the time, Anne Bass's horticultural interest was primarily in orchids, and Paul Rudolph had also designed an Orchid House some distance from the main house. But by 1983, her research, travel, and insatiable interest in gardens had led Anne to an interest in roses. "I didn't know much about roses at the time," she admits, "and less about herbaceous plants." Originally, neither architect nor landscape architect had planned a rose garden at the Fort Worth estate, so it is somewhat surprising that it gained the approval of both. The design approach of Russell Page, whose very name suggests traditional Old World European design, seems almost the polar opposite of the style of Paul Rudolph, one of the most austere modern architects.

Russell Page was invited to Fort Worth to look over the 86 by 115-foot plot proposed for the rose garden and herbaceous garden between the main house and the Orchid House. Today, Anne Bass remembers with affectionate good humor the first encounter with Page: "I think he was horrified at the very ultramodern house that Paul Rudolph had designed. He was, of course, as a traditionalist more used to the old houses of Europe."

One of the two challenges that Page faced—the aesthetic one—can be summed up in his own words to Anne: "I will get some charm into this place if it kills me." The second challenge was a serious horticultural one. Page wanted unusual trees, shrubs, perennials, and ground covers, but he also wanted plants that could withstand temperatures that fluctuated from 80 degrees one day to a sudden freeze the next, followed by summers of 100 degrees for days on end, often without a drop of rain. As always, Page was fascinated with the problem-solving aspect of his work and was equal to the challenge. Anne Bass's garden stands out as one of the best of his career, and it is his only Texas garden.

As Page worked at his garden plans in 1983–84, Anne had her own work; she continued to learn through reading, kept meticulous notes on the gardens she visited in her travels, and was always in touch with Page, who had become her new garden instructor, friend, and mentor. Anne remembers that he made her write out the plant order forms in Latin to make sure they received the right varieties and also, she suggests with a smile, "to make sure I was learning the correct names." Together they formed an impressive collection, including roses and herbaceous plants that would do well in the erratically changeable Texas climate (Zone 7 and occasionally Zone 6). They also accommodated their selections to the color palette that Page had chosen—one that is easily identified with Anne Bass's love of classical ballet: pale blues, lavenders, pinks, mauves, and white. Even in the selection of water lilies, the colors fall into the homogeneous color scheme. As in any good collaboration based on mutual

LEFT Anne Bass remembers the reasons
for some of Russell Page's choices: "He did not like
gardens that are divided into different types. The
roses should be mixed, because if one rose dies, you
are left with a hole." Color dominates the rose
garden as pink 'Tiffany' and 'Sweet Surrender' mix
happily with the bright red of 'Mr. Lincoln' and
the burnished apricot of 'Whisky Mac'.

PRECEDING PAGE A cloud of pink 'The Fairy'
Polyantha roses tumbles down the slope next to the
conically shaped althea shrubs, *Hibiscus syriacus*
'Blue Bird', which in summer are covered with
blue flowers.

OPPOSITE A band of soft blue outlines the water lily
pond and repeats the use of the Pennsylvania bluestone
that Page used for the elegantly wide stairway in the
background and the walkways between the rose and
the herbaceous gardens.

RIGHT Anne Bass holds 'Appleblossom', whose loosely
double blooms have the ruffled old-fashioned look of
a Redouté painting. Others on the ledge from her English
shrub collection include 'Perdita', 'Graham Thomas',
'Abraham Darby', and 'St. Cecilia'.

THE FAIRY

Polyantha

Polyanthas became known as "sweetheart roses" for their perfectly formed small pink buds. By the 1930s Polyanthas had been bred not only as tiny compact bushes that reached only 2 feet, but were then crossed with other roses of the day, eventually leading to the birth of the extremely popular class of Floribundas. The British hybridizer Anne Bentall chose to introduce the scrambling *Rosa wichuriana* into the breeding of the Polyantha. When 'The Fairy' was first offered in 1932 its advantage as a ground cover as well as a spreading space-filler immediately captured the rose gardener's attention.

The spreading growth habit of 'The Fairy' is different from the earlier, more compact, Polyanthas. While the individual blossom of 'The Fairy' is not particularly distinctive, the low-growing mounding shrub when completely covered with clusters of soft-pink roses makes it a superb ground cover in the Texas garden of Anne Bass. Planted 2 feet apart, 'The Fairy' fills the area without overcrowding. Its disease resistance and winter hardiness are pluses, and its glossy green leaves, appealing even when there are no masses of pretty pink blooms, make the kind of gentle yet bold statement this garden demands in order to complement the powerful Rudolph architecture.

respect, they each conceded to the other as, for example, when he refused to consider the idea of an all-white garden as being "too boring" for that place and this era.

Maintaining the garden since Page's departure has proved to be an extremely different sort of challenge. Susan Urshel and Paul Schmidt are the knowledgeable and dedicated husband-wife team who have tended the garden since its inception. Paul says "We've had roses die in a week because of the temperature change. We may find that the effect doesn't show until the following spring, when we discover even trees suddenly die in the summer because of earlier root damage." The first winter dealt the garden a tremendous blow: a hard freeze (the first in a century) devastated the garden. Everything had to be replanted, and what the visitor sees today is the same but more fully grown, thereby proving Page's original choices were good ones.

The garden sections are laced together by the hardscape—beautiful wide walkways of Pennsylvania bluestone. A favorite view of this garden is seen looking down from the pleached oak allée onto the space enclosed at the far southern end by a wall of nine Italian cypresses (*Cupressus sempervirens*) standing in statuesque European dignity to announce the farthest delineation of the garden.

Aside from in their own boxwood-contained section (*Buxus microphylla japonica*), roses are ingeniously used throughout the Bass garden. Behind the parterred Herbaceous Garden the strong, dark green foliage of 'Mme. Alfred Carrière' creates a patterned effect against a stone wall to be admired even when not in bloom. The strong arching canes of 'Sombreuil' and 'May Queen' are gracefully entwined among those of 'Mme. Grégoire Staechelin', whose foliage is a healthy, sturdy green. A pink cloud of 'The Fairy', a modern Polyanthus rose, creates a dazzling effect as it spills over the banks on both sides of the staircase. "And every Texas garden should have 'New Dawn'," declares Anne enthusiastically. "It is one of the hardiest and most dependable climbers."

In the eight irregularly shaped sections devoted exclusively to roses, color reigns supreme, albeit entirely mixed rather than in blocks of the same colors. The pastel colors of the overall garden picture are joined by the brilliant red 'Mister Lincoln' (Russell Page's favorite), the deep apricot 'Brandy', and even the bicolored 'Double Delight' among the Hybrid Teas. All have the highest ARS ratings (8 or higher). Likewise, the old rose section contains dozens of varieties, including 'Paul Neyron', 'Marchesa Boccella', and 'Blanc Double de Coubert' with the same high ratings. ❊

OPPOSITE White 'Iceberg' roses glow against a background of a favorite perennial, *Aster frikartii*, a plant native to the Himalayas.

ASIDE FROM IN THEIR OWN boxwood-contained section, roses are ingeniously used throughout the garden.

FORMALITY *and* GRACE *in the* MIDWEST

IN 1990, THE DAY AFTER THEY BOUGHT THE WOODLANDS, THEIR 8-ACRE PROPERTY IN LADUE, A ST. LOUIS SUBURB, CAROLE AND HAL KROEGER, EXCITED AT THE PROSPECT OF A NEW GARDEN, WERE OUTDOORS TALKING EXCITEDLY OF THEIR VISION OF THE FUTURE LANDSCAPE. THEY

agreed that the former garden should be exchanged for an open lawn framed by the magnificent collection of trees; decided what plants could be moved to a new perennial garden; and chose what needed to be terraced or leveled, and what steps and walls would have to be built. An important part of that vision would be a new rose garden to be placed between the house and the pool, the most trafficked area of the property.

John Cotta, who has maintained the garden since its inception and who had a hand in actually laying it out, says, "From the beginning they had a vision of how they wanted the entire property to look. It was amazing! Everything they mentioned that first day has actually happened the way they described." One of the Kroegers' top priorities was to preserve the woodland of oaks and hickories understoried by dogwood and redbud trees (*Cercis canadensis*), and particularly the Amur maple (*Acer ginnala*), near the rose garden. Changes in grading, however, would have to be made if

they were to have a rose garden, conserve all the trees, yet incorporate a large open grassy area where a tent could be set up for weddings and large parties, or where the Kroegers and their children could play badminton or Frisbee with the dogs.

Hal Kroeger, a highly successful businessman, studied architecture in college and has always been interested in landscape design. It was he who designed the rose garden, which he says was inspired by a combination of the rose garden of his childhood and the one at the St. Louis Botanical Garden. Carole, a painter whose work reflects a sophisticated handling of color, is also a knowledgeable horticulturist and hands-on gardener, and was responsible for choosing all the actual roses.

Straight rows with easy access to beds of Hybrid Teas and Floribundas was not what the Kroegers had in mind for their prizewinning roses. They have successfully reached their goal of arranging their collection of 273 rose

bushes in a way that is all at once orderly with easy access and yet aesthetically pleasing. Several factors influenced Hal's design. "The landscape has to relate to the house. We needed a passageway between the house and the pool and it seemed the ideal spot for our rose garden because it would be seen en route to the pool several times a day." He chose a circular shape because "it gives the maximum frontage of flowers and enables one to see them from each perspective, particularly as the sun moves. It also invites you to wander off course in a friendly way, yet it is symmetrical enough to be inviting."

Both Carole and Hal opted for a walkway of stone on the west-east axis. "We would have preferred a darker granite for the walls," says Carole, "but St. Louis white limestone was what was available so that is what we used." Guests interested in seeing the roses approach the garden from the lawn on the north-south axis, where one of the 3-foot-wide grassy paths bisects the

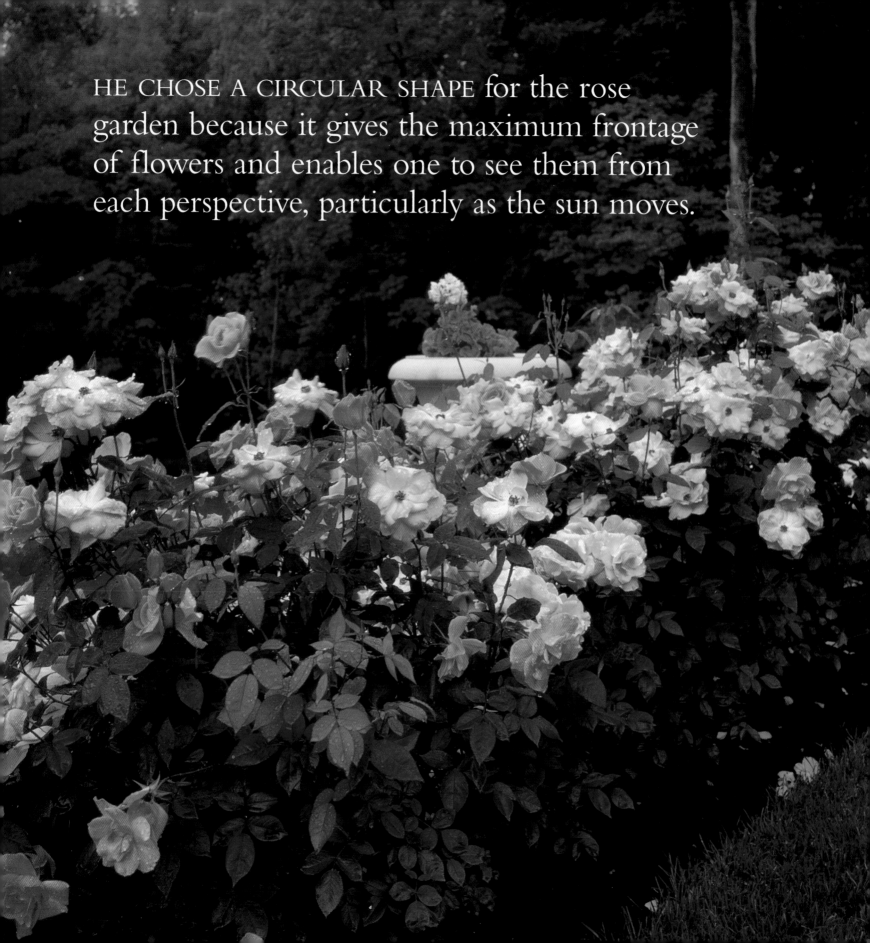

HE CHOSE A CIRCULAR SHAPE for the rose garden because it gives the maximum frontage of flowers and enables one to see them from each perspective, particularly as the sun moves.

circular rose garden and offers a pleasing vista of masses of roses in the foreground and the wooded area beyond.

The garden is laid out in three concentric circles. The innermost is divided into four strips of rose beds, one in each quadrant, the next circle has eight beds, and finally the outermost circle is made up of elongated beds forming a more continuous line, cut into four sections by the paths leading to the center of the garden. The well-thought-out perennial shade garden in the foreground serves as a harmonious preamble, in dramatic contrast to the perfectly placed 8-hour-a-day, sunshine-filled circle of roses just beyond the curving stone wall.

But no less impressive are the choices Carole Kroeger made in the roses themselves, chosen primarily for their disease resistance. Given this constraint, Hal adds with a certain pride in his wife's choices, "We have to be realistic in Missouri. It has got to be the toughest place in the country for growing roses. I am constantly amazed when I see these roses struggling yet still thriving despite the heat and the humidity."

Carole chose pink, white, and red 'Simplicity' Floribundas for the beds lining the entire outer circle next to the stone walls on one side and next to the yew hedge on the other. They bloom almost the entire year with very few disease problems. These balance each other on either side of the circle and are flanked by beds of modern Floribundas, 'Apricot Nectar' (apricot-pink), 'Iceberg' (white), and 'Bonica' (pink), to reinforce the harmony of colors.

The two inner circles are made up of twelve beds of colorful Hybrid Teas, each bed of the same variety, including the eye-catching reds 'Olympiad' and 'Mister Lincoln'. Carole says, "I wanted all pale peaches, pinks, and whites, but Hal said emphatically, 'If I can't have red roses forget the whole thing!'"

A beautiful design and a knowledgeable choice of disease-resistant roses are not the only reasons for the success of the Kroeger rose garden. It is the bed preparation, mulching, feeding, spraying, and ample watering programs that John Cotta has devised.

The lives of the Kroegers are filled with commitments to their family, to the community, and to Hal's very active business. Yet they have both successfully managed to include time in the garden—one of the most important interests they share together as a couple. ❋

PAGE 95 Once you have seen and smelled the 'Tiffany' rose at the Kroeger garden, you may wonder if there is a more perfect bloom in the world.

PRECEDING PAGES, LEFT Hal Kroeger designed the rose garden so it could be viewed from the bedroom. RIGHT Pink 'Simplicity' roses.

OPPOSITE Beds of pink, white, and red 'Simplicity' complete the circle of the rose garden.

TIFFANY

Hybrid Tea

'Tiffany' has been called the "royal successor to the Tea rose of yesteryear." Like the first Hybrid Tea, 'La France' of 1867, 'Tiffany' opens in a perfect swirl of petals, its remarkable fragrance coming forth with just a hint of lemon.

When 'Tiffany' was introduced in 1954 by hybridizer Robert Lindquist and the Howard Rose Company, it was awarded the Gold Medal. A year later it was named an AARS winner. 'Tiffany's' extraordinary fragrance was recognized in 1962 when it received the prestigious James Alexander Gamble Fragrance Medal. Peter Beales, the English rose authority, recommended the climbing version of this rose as one of the best roses of the 1950s. Since that time 'Tiffany's' rating has not been superior (7.3), although it continues to win prizes at the show table.

'Tiffany's' form, with a high, pointed center, should easily earn the required 25 points from American Rose Society judges in this important category. Its vigorous, upright growth and its elongated, perfect buds opening to large pink blossoms and framed by lush, dark green foliage are the characteristics that made Hybrid Teas so popular when they were first introduced. 'Tiffany's' glorious color certainly lights up any garden with a touch of gold at the base of each opening pink bud.

FOUR

SUN·BLESSED GARDENS *of* CALIFORNIA

Gold may have been the draw for the forty-niners who rushed to California in the last century, but it is the sunshine for days on end that continues to bring immigrants, vacationers, and professional rose breeders to the country's most populated state. The rose gardens in this section, stretching from northern California's Sebastapol 425 miles south to the more desertlike dry climate of Altadena, all enjoy the mild climate where winter protection is not even a consideration. All are blessed with consistent days of more than the required daily dose of 5 hours of sunshine. Special California microclimates like the Ojai Valley east of Santa Barbara, where the temperature drops to near freezing, allows Terri Campbell's Gallicas and Damasks to bloom as profusely as they do in colder areas of the country. ❈ In this section, several of the profiled roses emphasize the continuing evolution of the rose in modern times, including the Hybrid Tea, Floribunda, Hybrid Musk, and modern Shrub, all of which have made themselves indispensable in the landscape of contemporary American gardens. Many of the world's top hybridizers and rose growers call California home, as does Dr. Tommy Cairns, author and distinguished rosarian who, in addition to being twice editor of *Modern Roses* and president (as of 2000) of the American Rose Society, continues to document the evolution of America's favorite flower and believes as much evolution has taken place since the first Hybrid Tea as came before 1867. He cites as one example David Austin's English roses first produced in the 1950s, which brought the best of the old together with the newer Hybrid Teas, Climbers, and Floribundas, and which re-create the old garden rose forms with the capability of repeat blooms in a wide range of colors both old and new. Another innovation is in the color of roses: Sam McGredy IV of Ireland introduced the Hand-Painted series with 'Old Master'; also, there are bicolored roses such as 'Double Delight', voted "one of the world's favorite roses"; and the striped rose that first came on the market as a Miniature from Ralph Moore in California. One of these is 'Pinstripe', the grandparent of Tom Carruth's AARS winner Floribunda 'Scentimental'. Roses have continued to evolve as Miniatures, larger Miniatures known as Patio roses, hedges, and ground covers—each with a specific use in the American garden of today. In California, with its Mediterranean heritage and near-Mediterranean climate, garden designs may easily accommodate an abundance of roses. From rose gardens on a grand scale, such as Dolores Hope's garden for her husband, Bob, to cottage gardens to Lyn and Norman Lear's formal geometric garden by Dan Kiley, California is paradise for the rose.

A HYBRIDIZER in EDEN

WHEN TOM CARRUTH AND THE LATE JOHN FURMAN STARTED THEIR ALTADENA GARDEN IN SOUTHERN CALIFORNIA IN 1988, THEY WERE SELF-DESCRIBED "PLANT FREAKS" WHO HAUNTED NURSERIES FOR EVERY PLANT IMAGINABLE, INCLUDING ROSES. TOM, A HYBRIDIZER AND

Director of Research at Weeks Roses, and John, formerly a Professor of Theater and Humanities at California State Northridge, both wanted an attractive garden, not just a bed of roses. They enjoyed nothing more than finding new grasses, euphorbias, and heat-loving succulents that they mixed into their small city garden, which occupies two-thirds of the 60 by 140-foot lot.

Tom Carruth's reputation as a rose breeder is very much tied to the history of the Floribunda. Most Floribundas fit easily into almost any landscape, whether in the pastel tones of 'French Lace,' 'Origami', and the lavender 'Shocking Blue' or, as in the Carruth back garden where "hot colors" dominate the scene, in their outdoor garden living room where the loose, ruffly blooms of 'Champagne Cocktail', 'Playboy', and 'Scentimental' bespeak southern California more clearly than words.

Born, raised, and educated in Texas, Tom Carruth got his first opportunity to breed roses with the late Bill Warriner

of Jackson & Perkins, the company that, under the direction of Eugene Boerner (aka "Papa Floribunda"), helped make Floribundas today one of the most popular rose classes. At Weeks Roses, he has become one of America's most successful hybridizers of Hybrid Teas, Floribundas, and modern Shrub roses, including two 1999 AARS winners: 'Betty Boop', a yellow-edged red Floribunda, and the red-and-white-striped 'Fourth of July', the first Climber since 1986 to win the coveted award.

Although Tom Carruth has many AARS awards to his credit, he is especially proud of 'Scentimental', his 1997 award winner, one of the surprisingly few roses (fifty in all) found in his garden. 'Scentimental', with its burgundy-cream stripes, fits right into this garden: burgundy is the only consistent color in both the pastel front garden and the "hot color" garden behind the house. Tom and John felt the burgundy tone would add depth to the garden, and an overview of the area reveals touches of

it in purple-tinged mustard leaves, in the strikingly deep mauve New Zealand flax (*Phormium tenax*), and the very dark maroon succulents tucked in here and there. John Furman described 'Scentimental' with a good chuckle as "'Ferdinand Pichard' on steroids," and indeed it does resemble the two-toned Hybrid Perpetual of the 1920s—yet the newer version is more vivid and has more substance.

"There is a color scheme for the garden, and we always looked for plants to add to our collections that fit into that scheme," Tom reminisced. Even the bright orange Floribunda 'Orange Juice' finds a place and the bicolored Miniature 'Hoot Owl' holds its own in a riot of technicolor. John remembered with a laugh, "A lot of bright, contrasty color caused one visitor to call it 'the garden for the visually impaired.'" Bright colors bounce off each other and the eye is kept moving, since there is very little repetition of any one plant variety. Their collection of grasses—both native

BRIGHT COLORS BOUNCE off each other and
the eye is kept moving, since there is very
little repetition of any one plant variety.

and exotic—fits in handsomely with the euphorbias and sets off the roses in an unexpected way. The grass collection includes more than twenty varieties and gives a sense of place to this arid southern California garden in a way that few other plant families could do more effectively. Adding contrasting textures next to the roses are *Miscanthus sinensis* 'Morning Light' and 'Cabaret' along with the purple-leafed fountain grass (*Pennisetum setaceum rubrum*), which picks up the ubiquitous burgundy tone with a softness. Tom adds, "We particularly liked *Panicum virgatum* 'Heavy Metal', and found that the grasses go particularly well with the hot colors in the back garden."

Different sedges (*Carex* spp.) are another favorite collection: the needle-like leaves repeat those of the grasses, some fingerlike succulents, and the blades of daylilies and iris—all in strong contrast to the less distinctive foliage of the roses. The men shared an enthusiasm for the sedge and succulent families: "Each year we found a plant that would dominate in our collecting thoughts. It wasn't that we particularly felt those went well with roses, but rather just that a new plant came along that interested us. A dark red *Aeonium arboreum* 'Atropurpureum', for example, with its dark dramatic rosettes, is beautiful and stands up to even the most outstanding Floribunda rose." The variegated Japanese sedge (*Carex morrowii variegata*) is scattered randomly in clumps among the rocks next to the small man-made stream that recycles through the back garden. Other sedges include 'Blue Sedge' (*C. glauca*) and leatherleaf (*C. buchananii*).

It is difficult to remove a healthy plant from their small garden, but from time to time it was necessary as the pair's spirit of adventure and love of unfamiliar plants forced them to find new spaces for their ongoing collecting. John explained, "There is an inexhaustible collection of new things to try. If one is not replanting, one is not really gardening anymore. There is so much to discover." ※

SCENTIMENTAL

Floribunda

Dines Poulsen, the Danish rose hybridizer, is generally considered the patriarch of the modern Floribunda family. He and his brother, Svend, developed roses from the clustering Polyantha parentage into a new class called Hybrid Polyanthas in the early years of this century. For the next 30 years the Hybrid Polyanthas when bred with Hybrid Teas continued to grow taller and produce larger clustering flowers in a myriad of new colors that were noticeably different from their Polyantha parents. In the late 1940s, American nurserymen gave the class a new name: Floribunda. In the 1950s, other hybridizers were added to the history of the class: America's Eugene Boerner (also known as "Papa Floribunda") of Jackson & Perkins, England's Jack Harkness, both the Tantau and Kordes families of Germany, and Ireland's Sam McGredy. All produced beautiful roses that were a boon to landscape designers as hardy hedges, specimens, or anchors in a border.

Today the Floribunda is still a popular landscaping choice with the successful additions by Tom Carruth at Weeks Roses who continues to produce prizewinners such as 'Scentimental', a large double bloom of rich burgundy swirling with creamy white. It, like other Floribundas, is remarkably disease-resistant and, as its name suggests, is unusually fragrant.

HOLLYWOOD BEAUTIES

IN HOLLYWOOD'S GLORY DAYS OF THE 1940S, THE MOVIE ACTORS WERE IDOLS, THE STORIES ALWAYS ENDED HAPPILY, AND THE WOMEN WERE GLAMOROUS AND BEAUTIFUL. BOB HOPE, A BOX-OFFICE CHAMP OF THE DAY, AND HIS WIFE, DOLORES, MOVED INTO THEIR DREAM HOME

at Toluca Lake, near the Paramount and NBC Studios, in 1940. The 7-acre property had every Hollywood amenity, even a putting green, but it didn't have a rose garden. Thomas Church (1902–1978), one of the most outstanding California landscape architects after World War II, laid out the Hope garden, designed the beautiful flagstone terrace next to the swimming pool, and planted most of the trees that are on the property today. Still, Dolores Hope longed for roses to complete the picture.

Fifty years later, in 1992, Dolores Hope, a New Yorker, finally had the rose garden of her dreams. The 52 by 92-foot garden was inspired by one of her favorite gardens, Old Westbury, on Long Island, New York. "I tried to copy that garden and particularly the pergola as closely as possible, but I didn't want to take up too much space because we never knew how much room we would need for an event . . . or I would have had the whole area in garden."

At the suggestion of former First Lady Nancy Reagan and Betsy Bloomingdale, southern California friends who also had beautiful rose gardens, Dolores Hope chose Charles Follette, a graduate in Horticultural Sciences from the University of California at Berkeley, to help her with her first real rose garden. His horticultural expertise and specific knowledge of American and European rose gardens, along with his amiable personality, have made him one of the most sought-after rose garden designers in the Los Angeles area.

"Mrs. Hope was very knowledgeable about roses and had certain ones in mind she knew she wanted." With the exception of 'Queen Elizabeth', the classic Grandiflora of all times, her list included only modern Hybrid Tea roses, and each has been not only an All-American Rose Selection prizewinner (the highest award a rose can achieve) but also southern California favorites for decades: 'Duet', 'Pascali', 'Bewitched',

'Mister Lincoln', and 'Peace.' Others that make up the fifty varieties in the Hope garden were chosen by Dolores and Charles from Follette's Rose Garden Nursery in Santa Monica, when the nursery was in full bloom.

Several of the Hybrid Tea and Floribunda arching beds are dominated by shades of pink, white, and red. These stand out like lacy cutouts against the sand-colored paths of decomposed granite. Each bed is meticulously outlined by a thin border of grass that sets off the rose beds even more.

There are no gaps in this profusely blooming rose garden, which is reminiscent of a gorgeously oversized floral nosegay or even, appropriately, of a romantic 1940s valentine. Dolores, Hope's wife of more than sixty-five years, says with sincere devotion in her voice, "It is my garden for Bob."

Stretching the entire 90 feet of the garden on the southern side is one of today's most popular roses: 'Bonica', a

PRECEDING PAGE 'Sunsprite', a magnificent yellow climber with a high ARS rating (7.9), was formerly called 'Yellow Blaze'. In the garden of Dolores and Bob Hope it is one of several climbers that grow up the 10-foot-high pergola. A profusion of pink-blend blossoms cover the shrubs of 'Bonica' at the base of the arbor.

ABOVE Like an enormous valentine, the beds are cutouts in different geometric shapes fanning out according to height from the central bed of Floribundas and arranged in completely separate color blocks.

LEFT On hot summer days in Southern California a covered walkway under a rose arbor is a favorite place to enjoy the garden and smell the roses. Dolores Hope and Charles Follette designed the pergola to resemble one she had seen at Old Westbury, Long Island, New York.

OPPOSITE The red 'Olympiad' stands above masses of pink, red, and deep purple Floribundas of the innermost circle, and includes 'Cherish', 'Intrigue', 'Showbiz', and 'Sexy Rexy'.

BONICA

Shrub

Classified as a Shrub, this quintessentially modern rose first produced in France by Meilland in 1982 is also called a Landscape rose, a Patio rose, or even a Ground Cover rose. Whatever it is ("A rose by any name . . ."), 'Bonica' was the first Shrub rose to win the All-America Rose title. Its prolific small shell-pink blossoms, relatively easy care, and low-growing (3½ feet), spreading growth habit (5 to 6 feet) were all considerations when Charles Follette decided to use 'Bonica' as a space-defining boundary for Dolores and Bob Hope's Toluca Lake rose garden. Its disease-resistant, shiny, green foliage makes it a perfect hedge or low screen, and an ideal foil for its almost constantly blooming arching sprays. One recognizes its Polyantha ancestry in the clustering pink profusion of small blooms that give it an old-fashioned look.

Renowned rosarian Rayford Reddell gives it the highest praise: "'Bonica' is the first wave of tomorrow's roses—free blooming, disease-resistant, and not fussy over whether or not it's regularly pruned." It fits into the garden landscape so effortlessly and defies the notion that roses are difficult to grow. 'Bonica' is hardy in most parts of the country, but will die back to the bud union in Zone 4 and colder, only to come forth in the spring with perhaps the longest continuous flowering of any rose shrub today.

modern Shrub rose developed by the House of Meilland in 1987 and the first Shrub rose to win the AARS award. It is often listed either as one of the Meidiland Rose Series or as a "landscape rose."

'Carefree Wonder' is another pink modern Shrub rose in the Meidiland series with an ivory reverse on the profuse pink blossoms. Charles uses this extremely popular Shrub rose effectively in some of the red, white, and pink valentine beds. It, like its older sister 'Bonica', also received the coveted AARS award, in 1991.

Charles knew the arbor should not "just stick up out of nowhere." There is a gradation of heights leading to the structure beginning with Floribundas, then Hybrid Teas standing a little taller as the next arching beds, then some standard tree roses that are still taller. Finally, scrambling up the 12-foot-high arbor, is the single red Climber 'Altissimo', reaching over the top to meet the profusely blooming 'America', and in brilliant, sunny contrast is the yellow 'Sun Flare'. The pale pink blooms of 'New Dawn' come shortly after the two Climbing 'Cecile Brunner's at each end of the pergola, and the Large-flowered Climber 'Joseph's Coat' is a constant source of color for months on end.

In addition to arranging the roses by height, Charles wanted to structure the garden into color blocks: pinks, whites, and reds next to each other; pastel yellows, lavenders, and corals take up the next beds; and then apricots, oranges, and golds with some salmon are brought into the last beds. Paths fan out from the brilliant red central bed filled with 'Olympiad'. The radiating paths delineate exquisite trapezoidal, rectangular, and triangular beds filled with several classes of roses chosen for their height, color, compatability of growth habit, and fragrance wherever possible. From a practical point of view, Charles added, "I designed the beds so that you could have access from all sides and not have to actually get into the beds to smell the roses or to work in the garden. Each bed isn't so wide that you can't reach the center."

Since President Bush's visit the day after the garden was completed in 1992, countless guests have delighted in viewing the garden, but no one appreciates it more than its owners. Marveling at the beautiful display of roses as he strolled through the garden one afternoon, Bob Hope paused for a sniff of the very fragrant 'Intrigue' and smiled, "Wow! This is amazing! I guess I *did* promise her a rose garden." And it is definitely worth the wait of fifty years if you can have a rose garden as lush, beautiful, and perfect as the one Dolores Hope created with Charles Follette. ❋

OPPOSITE, ABOVE 'Dainty Bess', a distinctive, yet simple rose, is a rare single Hybrid Tea. Its stamens, a beautiful ruby shade instead of the usual yellow, contrast with dusky pink five petals.

OPPOSITE, BELOW Charles Follette, a botanist and horticulturist from the University of California at Berkeley, designed the Toluca Lake Hope garden in 1992 with Dolores Hope. He now keeps it in impeccable order.

BEAUTIFUL AMERICAN ROSE GARDENS

DOLORES, HOPE'S WIFE of more than sixty-five years, says with sincere devotion in her voice, "It is my garden for Bob."

NUANCES *of* WHITE

IN THE 1940S, WHEN THE MOVIES WERE THRIVING AND TV WAS IN ITS INFANCY, PAT McNAMARA WAS A DESIGNER WITH THE TOP HOLLYWOOD SET AND COSTUME DESIGNERS AT PARAMOUNT PICTURES AND HER LATE HUSBAND, EDWIN, WAS PRODUCTION DESIGNER FOR SOME OF MGM'S

major movies. This beginning led to another career for Pat and Ed, who for the past twenty years have designed, restored, or built from scratch and have decorated residential projects throughout southern California.

Their own Spanish Colonial Revival–style home in Pasadena, California, was designed in 1925 by Roland Coate, one of the most prominent southern California architects of the 1920s. When they acquired the ½-acre property across the street from the Huntington Sheraton Hotel (now the Ritz-Carlton), it had fallen into disrepair on a grand scale. The only separate residence Coate designed on the hotel grounds, it was intended for luxury guests.

The McNamaras updated the interior of the house with a soft beige-white palette reminiscent of Tuscan country houses, and decided to continue the same monochromatic flow into the garden. Easy maintenance, a hallmark of the southern California lifestyle, was another consideration.

If there is one word that characterizes Pat McNamara, it is *courageous.* When Edwin McNamara first saw the dilapidated house in 1986, it in no way resembled the resort cottage it had been, and for some time he could not share his wife's enthusiasm for such an enormous restoration. Pat's landscape and gardening training began in the 1960s, with Philip Chandler as her teacher and mentor at the University of California. "Chandler was a great teacher. He believed a garden should be peaceful and that this was accomplished by a repetition and a massing of plants. He also taught me that a garden must be beautiful even when there is nothing in bloom."

Garden walls are Pat McNamara's signature, for practical as well as aesthetic reasons. Her own 60 by 150-foot wall began with concrete blocks covered with plaster, and now stretches the entire length of the garden next to the street, blocking off noise and ensuring privacy. On the inside, the wall defines

the garden. As with the Mediterranean courtyard, the garden also offers passersby a glimpse through the front cast-iron gate.

Like the pergola, raised beds, and wall, the walkway was also designed by Ed McNamara. It is made up of irregularly shaped concrete slabs separated by various plants with silver foliage, including cranesbill (*Erodium chrysanthum*), snow-in-summer (*Cerastium tomentosum*), and silver thyme (*Thymus rugaris* 'Argenteus'). Santa Barbara daisies (*Erigeron karvinskianus*), blue star creeper (*Laurentia fluviatilis*), and white violets (*Viola odorata*) also fill the cracks between the stones, their small white flowers echoing in miniature the dominant white theme and adding at the same time a softening effect to the concrete stones. Peaceful shades of white and off-white in tones of creamy ivory, gray, and blue-tinged silver contrast with various shades of green foliage. Textures, flower shapes, and hues that are intriguingly compatible are stitched

ABOVE Pat McNamara has used the low-growing, 5-foot spreading 'Alba Meidiland' Shrub rose as a ground cover under Shasta daisies in the concrete-lined raised beds. A collection of gray-foliaged herbs and perennials keep the garden interesting long after the roses have gone by.

LEFT In addition to roses, white oleander splashes a hardy Mediterranean touch against the front gate. Concrete is used effectively as edging in the center beds, for the raised beds against the front wall, and for the path leading to the front door.

PRECEDING PAGE With no lawn to mow and cut-stone walkways, this front yard is easily maintained. The formality of the garden is achieved in part through the 'Iceberg'-covered pergola and the erect 'Iceberg' tree rose in an Italian stone pot at the northern end.

PEACEFUL SHADES OF WHITE and off-white in tones of creamy ivory, gray, and blue-tinged silver contrast with various shades of green foliage.

together harmoniously throughout the McNamara's garden.

The formality is built into the structure, with a large white pergola at one end and raised concrete beds behind the pergola on either side of the front gate. In the center of the garden, six rectangular beds section off diagonal rows of English lavender (*Lavandula angustifolia*), each of which is filled with lush Mediterranean herbs, native shrubs, and flowers. These are each centered with an 'Iceberg' rose and set off by underplantings of gray, white, and silver foliage chosen to look pretty throughout the year, ebbing and flowing as the seasons change and as new flowers come into their prime. A standard 'Iceberg' planted in an Italian stone pot stands in front of the pool at the northern end of the garden, and two Miniature 'Gourmet Popcorn' tree roses fill identical pots, adding balance at the southern end. Paths made of cut stones carefully color-matched to the house complete the color scheme established on the interior.

An equally heterogeneous planting is in the long 2-foot-high raised beds beneath the front wall. Here are numerous silvery-gray-foliaged plants, including *Cerastium tomentosum* and four species of *Artemisia,* whose textures play off one another (*A. schmidtiana, A. ludoviciana, A. caucasica,* and *A. arborescens* 'Powis Castle'). These are set off by the glossy green foliage of jasmine vines espaliered against the wall above the bed and white oleander splashing white blossoms at the front gate.

But it is the 'Iceberg' rose that dominates in this southern California garden. Pat knew these Floribunda shrubs and lovely Climbers were the best to make up the structure of her garden because they are "the workhorses of the garden." Pat says, "I adore white 'Icebergs'. They are such performers and all they ask is to have their heads in the sun, a good drink of water, and an occasional 'meal' of anything I have on hand. They are definitely 'low-maintenance.'" Joining her symphony of white roses for a few weeks in spring are the once-blooming, equally low-maintenance Species roses 'White Banksia' (*Rosa banksiae banksiae*), one of the first roses to bloom in southern California's early springtime. Their glossy green foliage adds greatly to the lushness of the garden for the rest of the year. Pat chose another landscape winner, 'White Meidiland', a fairly new Shrub rose (1987) and one of the hardiest on the market today. This exceedingly popular, disease-resistant, low-growing Shrub rose is repeated here and there in the raised beds as a luxurious white ground cover.

At once strong and quiet, bold and delicate, but always beautiful and peaceful, Pat McNamara's garden has succeeded in living up to the mystique of its setting: like the house, which is listed in the National Register of Historic Places, the McNamaras' garden is a first-prize winner of the Dry Climates Award, given by the City of Pasadena, for its "outstanding design and water conservation." ✺

I C E B E R G

Floribunda

'Iceberg', since its introduction in 1958, has remained the most popular rose in America, and one of the top ten roses in the world. Though classified as a Floribunda, 'Iceberg' shares many of the characteristics of the *Rosa kordesii*, a class that was named for Wilhelm Kordes, one of the greatest rosarians of all time and the only person to have developed a species rose. His father started the family nursery, Kordes Sohne, in Germany in 1887, and since that time the family has continued to produce outstanding hardy, beautiful roses.

First produced by Kordes Sohne, 'Iceberg', like the *kordesii* roses, fills a need for hardy roses. Its clear, white blossoms can be found in gardens from California to Maine, repeating their double blooms throughout the summer and abundantly covering shrubs, or as standards or as climbers, all three styles of which are imaginatively used in Pat MacNamara's southern California white garden. 'Icebergs' are not fussy about soil and will produce abundant white clusters with a blush of pink in cool weather; they resemble old-fashioned roses yet have the Modern rose form. The dark green glossy foliage makes a medium-tall hedge that is amazingly clean, having few blackspot or other fungal problems. If pruned low on the bush, these Floribundas can make excellent long-lasting and fragrant cutting flowers.

ROSE-STUDDED GEOMETRY

DAN KILEY, THE PHENOMENAL OCTOGENARIAN WHO IN 1997 RECEIVED THE PRESTIGIOUS MEDAL OF ARTS AT THE WHITE HOUSE, IS REFERRED TO AS THE "DEAN OF AMERICAN LAND-SCAPE ARCHITECTURE" AND DESCRIBED BY COGNOSCENTI AS AMERICA'S GREATEST LIVING

landscape architect. Responsible for more than 1,300 projects, from Kyoto to St. Louis and from Paris to Kansas City, he also designed the intimate garden of Lyn and Norman Lear in Los Angeles. Nowhere are his principles of landscape architecture more beautifully reflected, albeit on an intimate scale, than in this dramatic setting. High on a ridge, the property falls away on every side into the canyon below, and the views take in the Pacific Ocean to the west and stretch to downtown Los Angeles to the south. Kiley's vision of the garden is that it extends into infinity, and he has incorporated the magnificent views into the landscape picture at every opportunity: "The relation to nature in this case is more panoramic, rather than immediately under your foot."

The first thing Dan Kiley does when considering a new project is to "listen to the site" and to his clients. "You are not looking at the site in isolation. You are listening to the client in relation to the surroundings." Lyn Lear wanted a rose

garden, and although Kiley claims he is not an expert, he identified rose gardens with the kind of geometry and structure he believes all gardens should have. The challenge was to fit the rose garden into the scale of the total site. "Proportion and relationships have to be like the ski turn—correct," says Kiley, and indeed the perfectly sized 60 by 120-foot former tennis court space, delineated at each end with wisteria- and rose-covered pergolas, is exactly that: "correct." According to Dan Kiley, at the Lear home the main consideration was that there was not much ground space at all. It is quite small and therefore the house dominates the site.

Instead of an English cottage garden with masses of flowers or a Capability Brown–style imitation of nature (which Kiley abhors), the Lear garden is fully American. Nature comes right into the garden scene.

"Lyn loves roses. I might not have used roses like that, but I did because she wanted them." The individual roses

are to the whole as "the fingernails are to the body. All the elements are there, but they are modeled in an intimate way to form a strong total—like a suit of clothes." Since by his own admission Kiley is not a rose expert, he relied on Rios and Pearson, a Los Angeles landscape architecture firm, to help with the specific selection of varieties that do well in southern California. The nine rose parterres edged with paving stones each contain only five Hybrid Tea rose bushes, which provide the owners with cut roses for the house. Yet the landscape is breathtakingly enhanced by the careful placement of the square beds and a perfectly conceived geometric relation to the whole.

A particularly brilliant yet very simple use of paving stones turned on the diagonal and integrated with the grass continues the flowing interrelation of landscape elements. "The reason I love using the stepping-stones that way is that it doesn't block the natural flow of green. The grass and the stones are inte-

OPPOSITE: LEFT, CENTER, BELOW 'Grace de Monaco', 'Sheer Bliss', and 'Chicago Peace'.

THIS PAGE: ABOVE LEFT, ABOVE RIGHT, CENTER, BELOW 'Sweet Surrender', 'Tropicana', 'Just Joey', and 'Medallion'.

PRECEDING PAGE Elongating the garden with a profusion of white blooms against the green lawn, a strong line of 'Iceberg' Floribundas runs along the eastern side.

JUST JOEY

Hybrid Tea

In 1994, 'Just Joey' was acclaimed the World's Favorite Rose by the World Federation of Rose Societies. Introduced in 1972 by the British firm Cants of Colchester, it has continued to be a steady favorite by both gardeners and florists alike. This prizewinning Hybrid Tea is immediately recognizable by its remarkable color: the deep apricot center fades to a lighter orange blush at the edge of its ruffled petals. Its classic Hybrid Tea form is revealed as its 30 petals open from a deep orange bud that are already beginning to ruffle into a perfectly symmetrical blossom. What most amazes those who see 'Just Joey' for the first time is its enormous size. Others are impressed by its powerful fragrance, inherited no doubt from one of its parents, 'Fragrant Cloud'.

It grows well in most regions of the United States, with the possible exception of the very hot southern climate, and it is remarkably disease-resistant. Its glossy foliage is an attractive addition to an otherwise lackluster bush. Some gardeners consider its bush to be lanky and not particularly vigorous, and others findthe stems too weak to be a consistent prizewinner. But its long-lasting cut flowers make all its faults excusable, particularly in colder sections of the country, where it is almost always in bloom.

grated as one totality. And another thing . . . I don't want to cut a line through nature and cut it into pieces. Again it is a harmonious joining." The rhythmic, Mondrian effect with an almost "Broadway Boogie-woogie" beat enlivens the area, reminding the viewer of Kiley's Bauhaus training and his Modernist connections. This almost abstract approach is complemented by classical touches of parterres, Doric columns on the pergolas, the axis, the lawn, and the overall structure.

The garden was not large enough for masses of trees, one of Kiley's signatures, but the dense row of pines behind the pergola at the northern end separates the driveway from the garden. At the other end, the trunks of the jacaranda (*Jacaranda mimosifolia*) trees "echo the pergola's white columns and give a better sense of dimension and depth," Kiley explains.

The perfect carpet of green lawn shows how Kiley treats empty space as a positive element, connecting the pergolas. To bring out the horizontal element even more emphatically, a strong line of 'Iceberg' Floribunda roses runs along the eastern side and delineates the rectangular length of the garden with its profusion of white blooms. A strong contrast to the green of the lawn, the 'Icebergs' light up the darker area beneath the trees that blocks out the houses on the neighboring hillside.

Kiley insisted that fragrance be a major consideration in the choice of the roses and other plants: "Fragrance is one of the greatest senses in our bodies because it brings back history and nostalgia. Roses are one of the best sources for fragrance and offer an exciting opportunity to explore subtle variations of scents. I also used jasmine in the Lear garden. On a moonlight night the smell of flowers is entrancing and romantic."

All of the Lears' roses are Hybrid Teas and almost all have been prizewinners, from the oldest in the garden, 'Kaiserin Auguste Viktoria' introduced in 1891, to the AARS winners of the 1940s ('Charlotte Armstrong' and 'Peace'), the 1950s ('Sutter's Gold' and 'Garden Party'), the 1960s ('Bewitched' and 'Pascali'), the 1970s ('First Prize', 'Just Joey', and 'Medallion'), and the 1980s, when the garden was designed ('Brandy', 'Sheer Bliss', and 'Sweet Surrender').

Here, roses are grouped according to color: whites and creams in one bed, clear pinks in another, silvery pinks and lavenders in yet another. Tree roses of 'Pascali' and 'Peace' mark the center of the geometrical beds.

In the Lear garden, as in all his work, Kiley insisted on reflecting one of nature's laws, that of a "spatial continuity" from the interior to the exterior and from each part of the garden to the next. "The Lears' garden is a hanging oasis almost like a Tibetan space. It was so important to make it a jewel-like fabric." ❊

OPPOSITE Tree roses of 'Pascali' and 'Peace' mark the center of the rose-studded geometrical beds. All the selected roses—mostly apricots, pinks, and mauves—in this small rose garden have been AARS prizewinners over the years.

HOMAGE *to the* FOOTHILLS

UNLIKE THE CITRUS AND AVOCADO GROWERS IN OJAI, CALIFORNIA, WHO BECOME ANXIOUS WHEN THE TEMPERATURES DIP NEAR FREEZING, TERRI CAMPBELL IS PLEASED, FOR HER OLD GARDEN ROSES LOVE THAT SHORT-LIVED CHILL IN JANUARY, AND LIKE THE NEIGHBORING

avocado and orange groves, her collection of Gallicas, Damasks, Albas, Centifolias, and other old garden roses appreciate the nine-month growing season with the extended California sunshine and even the harsh August heat. To this arid climate in Zone 9 Terri only has to add water to make it a perfect spot in southern California for growing those types of roses normally associated with New Hampshire, North Dakota, and Washington state.

Over half of the 500 roses in Terri Campbell's 2¼-acre garden are old garden and Shrub roses. Though the roses are not arranged chronologically by classes, as many old garden rose collectors prefer, Terri's garden offers a unique firsthand history of the rose, since each plant is placed aesthetically rather than historically, and often is coupled with plantings that highlight its best features.

When Terri and her husband, Jim, bought their property in 1987, it was mostly covered with Bermuda lawn that they "are still fighting," says Terri. "It

was in 1992 that I began to be really serious about the garden. I planned a garden for the millennium." Her love of roses is not for the blooms alone. She takes particular delight in her Species roses, *Rosa sericea pteracantha* and *R. glauca*—wild roses whose beginnings are in prehistoric times. Terri grows both of them for the sheer showiness of their red thorns and stems . . . and for their connection with the past.

Following the Species roses, which come early in May and are among the earliest to bloom in the garden, Terri's collection of once-blooming old garden roses begins its extraordinary annual show. One would not be surprised to find Gallicas, Damasks, and Albas in hardier climates such as in New England, but to find them growing so lushly in arid southern California makes Terri Campbell's garden unique. In late May, as a grand finale to the old garden rose extravaganza, comes the striped 'Rosa Mundi' that often "sports back" to its well-known ancestor, thought to be the

oldest Gallica of them all, 'Apothecary's Rose' (*R. gallica officinalis*). The Gallica producing the largest blooms, 'Charles de Mills', nestles in among some Bourbons and Hybrid Perpetuals, along with what several rose experts call the best striped old garden rose ever, 'Camaieux'. 'Surpasse Tout', a lovely Gallica with deep rose-cerise blossoms, grows in Terri's garden as a vigorous 5-foot shrub with deep green leaves and a strong fragrance, both typical of this old European rose class.

Terri has worked hard to capture the genius of the place. Views of the Topa Topa foothills, a part of the Los Padres Mountain Range, are framed by the arching roses.

Acknowledging the southern California setting, Terri has introduced various drought-tolerant native grasses, shrubs, and trees. Blue oat and pampas grasses, New Zealand flax, silver-leafed eucalyptus trees, native ceanothus, and a palm tree spotted here and there, not only enhance the roses but also give this

LEFT With a clump of blue oat grass in front, thousands of blossoms of old garden roses color this section of Terri Campbell's garden, including the repeat-blooming Bourbons 'Honorine de Brabant' (striped and splashed with red) and the very large magenta blooms of 'Mme. Issac Perriere' behind.

BELOW Shown here with one of David Austin's crimson shrubs, 'The Dark Lady', Terri gives the extra watering that makes her rose garden so spectacular in late May.

PRECEDING PAGE Terri Campbell has trained the 1957 Meilland Shrub 'Cocktail' as a climber. Displayed on one of the three arches that create a fragrant tunnel effect, the lively bi-colored single blooms are geranium-red with a primrose-yellow at the base. Pointed buds open to clusters of single flowers against glossy, leathery foliage.'Joseph's Coat', an equally vibrant red-yellow climber is on the arch behind.

FOLLOWING PAGES Under an arch laden with the blossoms of both honeysuckle and the large red blooms of 'Dublin Bay' is a memorable, fragrant treat for guests at this Ojai Valley garden. Coreopsis, Mexican primrose, and iris complement the roses.

garden a distinctively California feeling. California poppies, lupins, and fields of coreopsis that have gone to seed reappear every year in Terri's fertile soil to color large areas and keep the weeds at bay. Terry explains, "The truth is roses are not always beautiful. What I am trying to do is paint with roses, and to make your picture beautiful you have to weave in other plants."

Terri's 'Autumn Damask' is the most fragrant rose in her garden and one that particularly enjoys the heat of the Ojai Valley in summer yet is hardy enough for the low temperatures in January. Most of the Damasks, including those developed in the 19th century—such as 'Hebe's Lip', 'Ispahan', and 'Mme. Hardy'—are in the subcategory of "Summer Damasks," blooming only once a year. 'Mme. Hardy' is particularly worth the wait, however, and has been cherished by many since its introduction in 1832. But Terri's favorite, 'Autumn Damask', belongs to the other subclass (with the same name) that blooms in the fall as well as in the summer, unlike all other old garden roses. Throughout the country it is this fall-blooming prizewinner that has often won Dowager Queen, the highest award for old garden roses in American Rose Society shows.

Although Damasks, like their companion old garden roses, don't demand excellent soil, they get it at Terri Campbell's. "That is why my 'Autumn Damask' grew to a six by six-foot healthy green mass from one November to the next."

Steve Jones, an acknowledged old garden rose expert, claims that the key to Terri's success is her soil preparation, which is free of amendments.

Terri's collection of 500 roses just begins with the Gallicas and Damasks. Her Hybrid Perpetuals, Chinas, Teas, and even the more modern Hybrid Musks continue her blooming history of the rose, which gets better and better each year. Terri explains, "It usually takes about three years for the old garden roses and two for the Shrubs to come into their full glory." Rose lover that she is, Terri even has a few moderns, including a section devoted to Miniatures, Floribundas, and Hybrid Teas.

This garden has never been laid out on paper. "It just keeps turning into something else. For example, we wanted a gazebo and we realized at the same time we couldn't just have a flat eucalyptus forest, so we made paths between the trees. All of a sudden I had beds to work with and then we had flax to balance the tall trees. And then I wanted some wildflowers and suddenly my husband came home with five California native bush poppy plants (*Dendromecon rigida*), and I asked myself, 'Where am I going to put those?' And it turns out to be the best thing in the garden! And then suddenly there are record cold temperatures and they freeze to the ground and they are gone . . . just like life. You have happy accidents and disappointments and you just keep going. That is what gardening has taught me." ❊

AUTUMN DAMASK

Damask

The eminent rose historian Dr. C. C. Hurst suggests 'Autumn Damask' might not have been brought back from Damascus with the Crusaders in the 15th century, as was believed, even though it is still romantically identified with that city. Although its parentage remains a mystery, Hurst suggests that the fragrant 'Autumn Damask' rose is distinctly different from summer-flowering or once-blooming Damasks. Also known as *Damascena bifera, R. damascena semperflorens*, 'Rose of Castille', 'Quatre Saisons', and 'Four Seasons', the same fragrant, twice-blooming rose had been introduced into Mediterranean gardens from Asia Minor. In some parts of the Spanish-speaking world the 'Autumn Damask' is called "The Alexandrian Rose," connecting it with Egypt and Persia through the Moors in Spain. The attar, or oil, of these roses has throughout the ages been appreciated both for its medicinal uses and its commercial value.

In addition to its historical connection, Terri Campbell in Ojai Valley loves the Damask rose for the same reasons it was appreciated centuries ago: the arching branches robed in soft blue-green foliage and its abundant medium pink ruffled blossoms centered with their bright yellow stamens, and most important its fragrance, which connects the 'Autumn Damask' of today with man's earliest gardens.

VIEWS OF THE Topa Topa foothills, a part of the Los Padres Mountain Range, are framed by the arching roses.

CALIFORNIA COTTAGE

STEVE HALSTED, A NATIVE CALIFORNIAN, HAD GARDENED AS A BOY WITH HIS FATHER AND CONTINUES TO BE AS PASSIONATE ABOUT GARDENING AS AN ADULT. FORTUNATELY HE MET A WOMAN WHO LOVED GARDENING AS MUCH AS HE DID AND MARRIED HER. "CAROLE AND I ARE

both 'heavy gardeners.' When we married it was a case of two gardeners getting together." Carole, too, had grown up with a gardening parent—her mother—in northern California and had created several gardens before she and Steve designed their Santa Barbara garden together. A year after their marriage in 1987 they bought a cottage on a ½-acre property, where they made a small 50 by 100-foot space into a garden, which, California style, stays ablaze with flowers most of the year. They laughingly admit that, like many serious gardening couples, "we have our worst fights in and about the garden."

While behind the house camellias, begonias, and ferns grow happily in a shadier area, it is their jewel-like front garden, partially enclosed by the original grape-stake fence of the 1950s, that stuns visitors with its dramatically colorful use of roses. Carole Halsted explains, "It is not a rose garden 'proper' but a garden in which roses predominate."

Carole's gift has been to balance textures and colors in a way that appears random yet is carefully considered. Bricks, in particular, define the bones of the garden and contrast with the softness of the plants as they set off and separate the various geometric beds. Three of the beds are triangular and of different shapes and sizes. All three contain Hybrid Tea roses and a variety of colorful annuals and perennials. Curving around the three triangles is a thin (1½-foot-wide) arching rainbow of low-growing perennials punctuated by Miniature roses of different colors. And finally, on the far side, a broad sweep of color fills the area beneath the fence and continues the scheme of colorful annuals, perennials, and citrus trees.

The Halsteds' favorite Hybrid Tea roses, grouped loosely together by color, come in both hot colors (gold, yellow, and coral) and a mixture of pinks and pink blends, such as 'Color Magic', 'Duet', and 'Bewitched'. To further enhance the roses and soften the stiff-

ness of the Hybrid Tea bushes Carole has loosely bordered the roses with annual flowering lobelias (*Lobelia erinus*), snapdragons (*Antirrhinum majus*), johnny-jump-ups (*Viola tricolor*), and forget-me-nots (*Myosotis* spp.). Elsewhere, scabiosa, iris, calendulas, and poppies—both Iceland (*Papaver nudicaule*) and the bright orange California variety (*Eschscholzia californica*)—are arranged between loosely ruffled and brilliantly colored Floribundas 'Playboy', 'Playgirl', and the white 'Class Act' in a long perennial bed next to the back fence. The taller Floribunda 'Flutterbye' with its various shades of yellow is a newer addition to the colorful rose display in the back bed. Carole loves trying different flowering annuals every year, but Iceland poppies, pansies, calendulas, and larkspur are always brought in though not always in the same place.

A bed of 'Iceberg' encircles a birdbath placed so that bird-watchers at the breakfast table can enjoy the early-morning feeding and bathing in full

"IT IS NOT A ROSE GARDEN 'PROPER' but a garden in which roses predominate. We brought our favorites with us and made the garden around the roses we both loved."

view. In the circle a small birdhouse perched on a post is daintily covered with one of the most successful of the fairly new Hybrid Musk class, 'Ballerina'. The apricot 'Buff Beauty', 'Lavender Lassie', and 'Clytemnestra' are other examples in the garden of this modern class with an old-fashioned look.

When the first flush of roses comes forth in late April and early May the coastal morning fog doesn't always burn off until late afternoon, and the temperature almost never rises to the eighties as it might later in July and August. These conditions have produced a new phenomenon that perplexed the Halsteds: downy mildew. Until 1994 Steve and Carole Halsted, like other experienced Santa Barbara rose gardeners, had never heard of downy mildew. At first they didn't recognize what it was, but they soon learned that if the infestation is not stopped the plant eventually dies. Although the Halsteds are loath to spray, they learned that for downy mildew there really is no choice. They, like many rose growers with a problem, turned to Dan Bifano, one of southern California's most experienced Consulting Rosarians who can usually explain symptoms, offer remedies, and give encouragement.

In addition to the repeat-flowering Hybrid Musks, Ramblers and Large-flowered Climbers decorate the surrounding white lattice fence, and the entrance arbor is at times heavy with the blooms of Climbing 'America'. Because the area is so small the Halsteds have made great use of Climbers: 'Cecile Brunner' climbs the stairway to the upper story and scrambles over the living-room roof. The massive blooms of a climbing 'Peace' on the other side of the front door are perfectly in scale with the flowers of the trumpetvine in which it is entwined, and the single pink blossoms of 'Sparrieshoop' create a glorious display as its climbing branches reach over the garage and bask in the full sun.

When Steve lived in Los Angeles he attended gardening classes offered at UCLA by Philip Chandler and it was at that time that he learned most about plant identification and plant diseases through the class field trips to local gardens and nurseries. Carole, too, attended horticulture classes at the Santa Barbara Botanic Garden. More recently, Carole has turned her leisure-time hobby into a profession and has been a garden designer since 1992. Although her career has taken off, her own garden still remains an important part of the life she shares with her husband. ❈

BALLERINA

Hybrid Musk

The Reverend Joseph Pemberton is given credit for introducing the first Hybrid Musk rose in 1918, and for a while they were called Pemberton roses. After that, the rose gardening couple John and Anne Bentall produced many popular Hybrid Musk roses, introducing the beautiful repeat-blooming shrub 'Ballerina' in 1937.

Hybrid Musks include *R. multiflora*, *R. moschata*, Ramblers, Polyanthas, Noisettes, Hybrid Teas, and Tea roses in their varied background. Because of this diverse heritage there is a wide range in height from very short (3-foot 'Autumn Delight') to very tall (6- to 8-foot 'Kathleen'). All are recurrent, however, mostly fragrant, and have long trusses covered with blooms that can be either single or multi-petaled.

'Ballerina' is the landscape designer's delight as an eye-catching shrub when in bloom and has dark green foliage and tiny, decorative hips. It grows comfortably to 4 feet, and though it likes to spread its arching canes, it can be trained into a small standard, or as a pillar rose as the Halsteds have done. It grows easily in cold climates (to Zone 5) with some winter protection. At the other end of the temperature scale 'Ballerina' performs equally well, tolerating heat up to Zone 10. Its disease resistance, particularly in a humid climate, is remarkable. 'Ballerina's' small single pink flowers with white centers remain a deeper pink longer in semishade.

PAGE 131 Apricot 'Just Joey', white 'Iceberg', the vibrant pink-blend of 'Color Magic' and the taller pink 'Duet' are tied by a curving ribbon of perennials and mini roses. 'Sparrieshoop' climbs rampantly over the garage roof.

OPPOSITE Shown here growing next to pink viburnum, the lovely Grandiflora 'Tournament of Roses' is part of an inspired arrangement that landscape designer Carole Halsted put together in her garden.

PRECEDING PAGES Chosen for their contrasting textures and complementary colors, veronica, snapdragons, heliotrope, astors, salpiglossis, and candytuft are mixed in with a selection of roses.

PRESERVATION *for the* FUTURE

EVEN FOR KNOWLEDGEABLE ROSARIANS, A WALK IN THE GARDEN OF PHILLIP ROBINSON AND GREGG LOWERY LEADS TO A DISCOVERY. THEIRS IS A GARDEN BASED ON A COLLECTION OF MORE THAN THREE THOUSAND ROSE VARIETIES—TWO-THIRDS OF WHICH WERE IN CANS

waiting to find a new home in 1986, when the men acquired the 2⅓-acre property in Sebastopol, California.

Some gardens evolve organically; some are planned to the last plant. Since 1989, when the garden was first laid out, at least 1½ acres have been planted as it was initially conceived. By 2000, their entire property will be a developed garden.

In their design of the garden, Phillip and Gregg had several concerns: the preservation of the collection, the health of the roses, and the garden plan that would show their roses to their best advantage. "Our main purpose was to figure out how to group these many different types of roses in a way that was sensible to us and from an aesthetic point of view as well." Miriam Wilkins, the founder and the chief organizer of the Heritage Rose Society, says of the Lowery-Robinson garden, "They haven't overlooked anything. Unlike many rose gardens it looks like a *garden*! It is not just in rows."

Gregg and Phillip believe there is a common misconception that *all* old European roses are older than the 19th-century hybridized roses. Gregg explains quite simply, "Look at the dates of the particular varieties from 1825 to about 1880. All the once-blooming old European roses and the reblooming Bourbons, Portlands, and Hybrid Perpetuals are parallel in terms of their development in the 19th century. However, the distinguishing feature is their ability to rebloom." This makes an easy, logical way of dividing the roses into at least two different rooms at the Lowery-Robinson garden and has an important aesthetic impact at the same time. "You can get the full glory of the once-bloomers if you pack them in together and you tend to thin down the glory of the repeat-blooming roses when you mix them with the once-bloomers."

Another consideration in the garden layout had to do with their personal enjoyment of the collection. While on

the one hand they knew that certain roses would grow best in specific parts of their property, which slopes from south to north, nevertheless they did not always put the roses in their optimum growth spot for a variety of reasons. Gregg allows that concessions had to be made. For example, the old European and Species roses would have been happier at the bottom of the garden where, when the temperature drops, the likelihood of setting good blooms is increased. But the owners' enjoyment of the roses took precedence and these sections were positioned in the upper garden near the road. "Since these roses have a shorter period of bloom than the other roses in the collection, we chose to put them in a spot where we spend less time, near a road which is fairly well traveled and consequently the noisiest part of the garden." The reblooming roses are planted together in a more prominent location.

A third consideration was to take advantage of the property's spectacular

BARONNE PRÉVOST

Hybrid Perpetual

Phillip Robinson describes the popularity of the 19th-century Hybrid Perpetual class as the equivalent of modern Hybrid Teas in popularity. One needs only to see and smell the blooms of 'Baronne Prévost' to understand why Hybrid Perpetuals were appreciated in the Victorian era and why, although one of the earliest in the class (1842), they remain a favorite today, both as a cut flower and at the show table.

In his 1991 article for the Heritage Rose Foundation Conference, Robinson reminds us of the great role Hybrid Perpetuals played in the establishing of rose competitions. 'Baronne Prévost' was among the prizewinners then as it is today. Its rich pink old-fashioned blooms tinged with lilac are consistently large (often up to 4 inches across), flat, and swirling with perfect symmetry around a green button eye.

Portlands, Damasks, Bourbons, and Hybrid Chinas all led to the first Hybrid Perpetuals and are evident of the hybridizing mania that went on in the second half of the 19th century.

Dean Hole, an early English authority, suggested Hybrid Perpetuals should have kept the former French name, *Hybride Remontant,* because they don't really flower "throughout the summer and . . . few resume their former glory in autumn." Nevertheless, Gregg Lowery believes 'Baronne Prévost' blooms more than most other Hybrid Perpetuals and its hardy, healthy foliage on a beautifully shaped shrub make it a garden favorite.

views: "My biggest concern was to take advantage of the view from our slope. It is very beautiful throughout the year, and we laid out a number of very long pathways that point toward the view. The gardens, in fact, are strung out along those pathways."

The double curved walls of roses are particularly dear to the owners. They serve as a backdrop for other parts of the garden and also work as an area-defining structure. But, more important, "it is exciting to walk through the climbing walls that rise on both sides of you." They wanted the experience of walking through a pergola but without the roof overhead, which can create an oppressive, damp feeling. Three pergolas are placed at the beginning, middle, and end of the curve, creating the impression that no end is in sight, and by having no ceiling other than the blossoms, the walk creates the sensation of being enveloped by the fragrance, texture, and lightness of the blooms.

More climbing rose walls will define the double mixed borders scheduled by the year 2000. The specific plants have not been chosen, but will include perennials, bulbs, annuals, shrubs, some evergreens material, and, of course, more roses. The scheme will be organized on a progression of flower color, and though it is Gertrude Jekyll inspired, it will definitely have a California feeling. "The intent is not to give the perennial beds a period quality but to create an exuberant planting that has value throughout the year," say the owners. The beds will move from the hottest tones to the coolest tones and finish at the bottom of the garden with a long horizontal white border.

A particularly spectacular section of the garden is the quadrant of modern Hybrid Teas and Floribundas, many of which are no longer grown commercially but are available through Gregg Lowery's Vintage Gardens Nursery. The shape of this section, a quarter of concentric narrow bands, was dictated by the site, but it seems utterly natural in the landscape. As long as this valuable collection of the loved, the once-loved, and the not-forgotten roses of yesterday are in the caring hands of Gregg Lowery and Phillip Robinson, they will be preserved for future generations of rose lovers. ❀

PRECEDING PAGE Planted in harmonious color drifts on the north sloping hillside, the Lowery-Robinson collection of Hybrid Teas includes those that, though still beautiful, are of another era. Because they are no longer considered fashionable, many are difficult to find, except at Lowery's Vintage Gardens Nursery in Sebastopol. A double curved wall of climbing roses serves as a backdrop.

LEFT This bouquet of Old Garden Roses includes the Hybrid Perpetuals 'Mme. Victor Verdier', front and center with 'Clio', the large pink above it, and the deep-red 'François Coppée' nodding below. Others completing the old garden rose bouquet are the beautiful white Alba 'Mme. Plantier', a pink 'Single Chestnut Rose' in the upper right, and 'Carnea', the very double blush pink left of 'Mme. Victor Verdier'. A cluster of 'Mary Washington' fluffy white Noisettes touched with pink is on the right.

BELOW Gregg and Phillip have preserved a magnificent view through the Old European Rose collection of Gallicas, Albas, and other once-bloomers through the arches to the landscape beyond. Here the spectacular section of Bourbons, Portlands, and other repeat-bloomers of the 19th century are grouped with iris and other perennials.

FOLLOWING PAGES
LEFT Hybrid Perpetuals and Bourbons begin to color this section of the garden in early spring.

RIGHT The single blooms of the 'Chinese Wilson's Rose', *Rosa sinowilsonii*, grow in clusters of large 2-inch white flowers. Even more distinctive are its leaves—the largest in the rose world—that can measure over a foot in length, and whose stems and new young leaves are a luminous ruby-red.

"YOU CAN GET THE FULL GLORY of the once-bloomers
if you pack them in together and you tend to thin down
the glory of the repeat-blooming roses when you mix
them with the once-bloomers."

FIVE

The NORTHWEST PASSAGE

In the first decade of the 20th century American gardens in the Pacific Northwest, as well as in the rest of the country, were beginning to take on their own distinctive flavor in which roses played a large part. In Portland, Oregon, the gardens did not follow any particular European tradition but simply embellished the favorite architecture of the day—modest or grand—Victorian, Italianate, Stick, Queen Anne, Gothic Revival, or merely a country farmhouse pared down to its simplest form. Blueprints, lumber, instructions for assembling, and even the required number of nails were sometimes mail-ordered from catalogues as "house kits," some of which were patterned after the most fashionable architecture of the day. ❁ By the time Portland, the first major city in the Pacific Northwest, was settled in 1844, the East Coast already had 300 years of American history under its belt. It didn't take long, however, for the Northwest to catch up in terms of beautiful estates and gardens. By the end of the 19th century the intercontinental railroads were completed and the Alaska Gold Rush of 1898 had enticed an even greater number to explore the Northwest's natural resources: gold, silver, copper, and especially timber. ❁ As the wealth poured into the newest area of the United States at the turn of the century, the lumber barons and their wives, along with the Olmsted brothers, who designed dozens of gardens in Portland, Seattle, and Spokane (the boomtown of the 1890s), had all discovered the joy and ease of Northwest gardening. Everything—and especially the rose—grew more quickly and easily than in any other place in America. ❊ Warmed by the mild ocean air in USDA Zone 8, Oregon and Washington coastal areas enjoy relatively warm winters compared to other American cities on the same latitude, like Bangor, Maine, and Duluth, Minnesota. ❊ Portland, in the Willamette Valley, is blessed with slightly warmer summers than on the coast. An annual rainfall average of around 37 inches, the most fertile soil, and the longest growing season in the area all contributed to the rose's becoming the most fashionable flower in the Northwest in the 1920s and later to Portland's being named the "City of Roses." ❊ But all is not mild in the Northwest. Cold winds often blow down from Alaska and Canada across the Puget Sound, lowering the temperature by twenty degrees in a few hours, dehydrating the plants, and making rose growing a little more difficult than along the coast. ❊ The climate in Spokane presents another weather challenge. Some 300 miles inland from the coast, Spokane has temperatures that dip three zones lower. In Zone 5, however, the second-coldest area in the West, winter dormancy ensures hundreds of spring blooms as long as the roses are tough. Here, rose culture and choice of roses has more in common with the Great Northern Plains, from Montana to North Dakota, than with the coastal areas of the Pacific Northwest.

OPPOSITE   'JOHN F. KENNEDY'—AS PURE A WHITE AS THEY COME—FROM THE KROEGER GARDEN IN ST. LOUIS.
PRECEDING PAGE   FROM THE CANADIAN EXPLORER SERIES, 'JOHN CABOT' IN GERRY KRUEGER'S GARDEN IN SPOKANE, WASHINGTON.

OREGON TURN-*of-the*-CENTURY CHARM

WHEN DANNY HILLS AND WAYNE HUGHES FOUND AND BOUGHT THEIR 1899 HOUSE ON A 1-ACRE CITY LOT IN THE WOODSTOCK NEIGHBORHOOD OF PORTLAND IN 1988, ITS UTTER ABANDONMENT WAS REFLECTED IN THE BOARDED-UP WINDOWS, CAVED-IN WRAPAROUND FRONT

porch, and particularly the yard, a dump filled with junk of every description, including rusted automobile parts, tires, and miscellaneous unwanted refuse thrown into the bushes by passersby.

Undaunted by the enormity of the task before them, Danny Hills, an artist and designer turned garden architect, and his partner, Wayne Hughes, a skilled carpenter, restored the rustic turn-of-the-century farmhouse to its former dignity (as funds and time permitted) and have developed the garden in a way that echoes the feeling of the house and the era in which it was built.

Early on, Danny did a little garden archaeology and found to his delight, once the bramble had been removed, that a Climbing 'Cecile Brunner' and a 'Dr. W. Van Fleet' Rambler planted long ago were still alive, having been shaded by the canopy of an overhanging filbert tree that the owners believe had probably been planted by a squirrel. These roses, with a few bearded iris rhizomes, appeared to be the only vestiges of the garden that might have existed early in

the house's history. The trunk size alone suggested that the 'Dr. W. Van Fleet' was at least seventy-five years old. Danny dug up the rose, pruned it, and moved it to a spot in full sun. Today the large pink-fading-to-white blossoms annually cover almost everything in sight.

According to Wayne, Danny's goal for the design of the garden was "to maintain that original farmhouse crudeness. There would be no ornate flower bed edging and Willamette Valley fieldstones would stand in place of the wrought-iron garden structures one usually identifies with Victorian design." In addition, they wanted a garden that would be ecologically sound and so healthy that no spraying would be necessary. Wayne explained that during that first spring bloom, when they saw their newly planted Rugosa rose 'Roseraie de l'Hay', which was so much fuller and so much stronger than the other four Hybrid Teas they had planted at the same time, they knew right away that they only wanted "no fuss" roses that were disease resistant.

Their garden now boasts 200 roses, but in the beginning, Hills and Hughes admit, they knew practically nothing about the species. During the first long rainy winter they devoured rose books from the Portland public library, and soon determined that the Kordes, Rugosas, Hybrid Musks, and Canadian Explorer series would be the rose families that would predominate in their garden. Space had to be found for other old and modern Shrubs (the spectacular white 'Sally Holmes' and 'Lyda Rose', and 'Sparrieshoop' and 'Shropshire Lass', both pinks) simply because they all had the right feeling for their "blowsy, casual" garden. As they continued their research they also learned that all the Climbers—the Large-flowered ones like 'Dr. W. Van Fleet', the creamy white clusters of Multiflora Ramblers like 'Bobbie James' and the bright red everblooming Kordes 'Dortmund'—would be beautiful vertical additions. Their trial-and-error approach continues with the result that the garden is a rose laboratory in constant flux as some varieties

BOBBIE JAMES

Rambler

Ramblers are usually described as "once-blooming, small-flowered climbers." 'Bobbie James' falls into the sub-group called *Multiflora* Ramblers, reflecting its relationship to the Japanese species rose. Most Ramblers are so vigorous that, if left unpruned, they will cover everything in sight and become a thorny menace. Yet, more often than not, 'Bobbie James' and *Multiflora* Ramblers in general can be the most beautiful and dramatic addition to the garden. The lax, freely arching canes are covered with draping clusters of small, old-fashioned cupped blossoms, giving the impression that they belong to a much older class of roses, though most were not produced until the dawn of the twentieth century.

'Bobbie James' is an even more recent addition. It was named by Graham Stuart Thomas in 1961 for his friend and fellow rosarian, the Hon. Robert James. 'Bobbie James' is appreciated not so much for its panicles of beautiful small white blossoms and glossy pale green leaves, but for its many uses in the garden. More often than not, 'Bobbie James' is listed as a tree climber because of its ability to stretch at least 25 feet into far-reaching branches. It is also the ideal rose for covering pergolas, arbors, trellises or even unsightly buildings. With support, it grows beautifully as a free-standing pillar rose.

are taken out and others are added. At the same time, they have begun to collect perennial flowers and shrubs with the same enthusiasm as they cultivate their roses.

In the beginning the beds were planned around a spot where one of Danny's marvelous handcrafted birdhouses could be shown to advantage. The birds seemed to appreciate the architecture of the houses and were immediately drawn into the garden, where they continued to carry out the owners' ecological plan: they devoured thrips and other harmful bugs while their droppings added nitrogen to the soil.

Danny confessed, "At first I thought all old garden roses were disease free and hardy. Later I learned that one should look at the rose parentage to find the particularly hardy ones. And still, despite what is written about them, certain ones just don't work in our garden and have to be removed." They have continued through the years to buy most of their roses from Louise Clements of Heirloom

Old Garden Roses in nearby St. Paul.

Both Danny and Wayne love the rainy Portland winters when they have time to read, learn, build birdhouses and custom garden structures, and to enjoy their garden from a new perspective. Danny explains, with an engaging appreciation for what they have, "I want to be able to see the rock wall we built when we began the garden because we don't see it in the spring and summer. Birdhouses and fences look wonderful in the winter and the structures and occasional finials we've found from an old porch are seen only at this time. With snow on them, the supporting structures of willow wood and the few architectural pieces look wonderful." He adds philosophically, "I really don't care whether the roses are repeat bloomers or not. There is a cadence to life. Some people try to keep spring going too long. The garden should have a magnificent flush in spring that makes your heart hurt. Then it is ready to go to sleep. Winter brings new delights." ❋

OPPOSITE, ABOVE Even blooms that have past their prime still maintain their shape such as the pink 'Eden'. Shown in the foreground the dried blooms are allowed to hang on in the garden as reminders that all stages of a rose are part of nature's beauty. In the background the vigorous 'Bobbie James' rambles more than 25 feet when given the support and the rain of the Pacific Northwest.

OPPOSITE, BELOW A view of the garden showing some of the numerous birdhouses made by Wayne Hughes, a skilled carpenter. He and his partner, garden designer Danny Hills, developed the garden in a way that echoes the feeling of the 1899 Willamette Valley farmhouse and its era with loosely connected drifts of blowsy roses and Victorian perennials that do well in the Portland area.

PRECEDING PAGE "Kordes roses are our favorites," both Danny and Wayne agree. Here the single red 'Dortmond' is disease free, repeat blooming, and very hardy. On the fence in front of the Victorian house restored by Hills and Hughes, bright red 'Dortmond' and delicious pink 'Dapple Dawn' roses next to purple clematis and tall pink malva greet visitors at the front gate and cheer the passersby.

DEEP-FREEZE BLOOMS

SPOKANE, WASHINGTON, IS 300 MILES EAST OF SEATTLE AND NEAR THE ROCKY MOUNTAINS, AND ITS CHILLY CLIMATE IS EQUALLY DISTANT FROM SEATTLE'S MILD, RAINY, GARDEN-FRIENDLY WEATHER. SPOKANE HAS EXTREMELY COLD WINTERS (−20 DEGREES IS COMMON),

summer temperatures climb over 100 degrees, and the average rainfall is 14 inches a year. Who would *think* of growing roses in that kind of climate? Gerry Krueger figured out how to grow roses naturally, and she has done it for years. In fact, Gerry's friend Bill Grant, the noted rose historian, calls her "The Rose Lady of the North."

Gerry's garden got started with her grandfather's homestead rose from Rose Lake, Idaho, and a few old garden rose cuttings from Canada in 1983.

To those first old garden roses other hardy roses were added, including fifty Ramblers and *R. wichuriana* hybrids, and more than two dozen Species roses, all of which performed so well on the Krueger 22-acre farm that soon a mail-order nursery, Blossoms and Bloomers, filled the desperate needs of thousands of climate-challenged rose lovers. "I only had seventy varieties, but they were roses you couldn't get anywhere else." She started with orders from Montana, Idaho, North Dakota, Wyoming, north-

ern Minnesota, and Alaska, but soon she had orders from all the other states—Florida included. Her mail-order business of hardy perennials and own-root roses flourished until Gerry decided after seven years to close that side of her business and sell only to those who visit her garden nursery in Spokane. Today, other reliable mail-order resources sell the "tough roses," as Gerry Krueger calls those in her garden: the Explorer series, Gallicas, Damasks, Albas, Rugosas, and certain hardy Species roses.

Over the years, the Kruegers have dedicated themselves to the preservation of native flora and fauna. Recently, the Washington State Department of Conservation turned 17 of the original 22 acres behind the Kruegers' 3-acre garden into a wildlife preserve. Through a wildlife conservation grant from the state, the preserve has been planted with native shrubs and trees.

For a garden that got its start as recently as 1983, it is remarkably mature: roses clamber over the barn walls, curl

around arbors, and stretch to the sky in billowy pink and white pillars. "That shows how fast the old roses grow," says Gerry modestly. She is similarly humble about her cultivation techniques; she declares she never fertilizes or waters once the new roses are established, never sprays, and prunes "only when they get so big they attack me." As for winter protection, she scoffs: "I do no winterizing! If I had to bend and cover the roses as in the "Minnesota tip" or wrap my roses in burlap, it would be spring before I finished. I don't do a big cleanup in the fall because I am too busy propagating in my greenhouse and don't have time."

Here, the roses dictated the original garden design. Gerry never laid out her garden on paper, but her prior training as a graphics designer and artist helped her place her unusual hardy perennials so that they would enhance the roses.

Each year Gerry brought new structures (all from recycled lumber) to the garden and shaped it into a never-quite-

MAIDEN'S BLUSH

Alba

Only superlatives can be used when describing the Alba class, and 'Maiden's Blush' is one of its best examples. Graham Thomas once wrote, "The White Roses (Albas) are supreme over all the other old races in vigour, longevity, foliage, delicacy of colour, and purity of scent." 'Maiden's Blush' is among the earliest of the old European roses. Its origins predate the 15th century, and it was most likely created by a crossing of *Rosa damascena* and the species *Rosa canina*. The French have more suggestive names for 'Maiden's Blush', such as 'Cuisse de Nymphe Emue' (literally "thigh of a blushing maiden"), 'La Seduisante' (the Seductive One), and 'La Virginale'.

All Albas are not white as its name would imply, yet the color range never goes beyond a mid-pink. The very large multi-petaled blooms of the silkiest blush-pink 'Maiden's Blush' are often so profuse they completely hide the saw-edged gray-green leaves that are characteristic of the class.

'Maiden's Blush' is also celebrated for its disease resistance and its hardiness, surviving with absolutely no winter protection. Its amazing tolerance of shade caused Thomas to suggest it for growing on a north wall. But perhaps the most important characteristic for many rose connoisseurs is its delicious scent. As Thomas once wrote, There is no rose scent so pure and refreshingly delicious as that of 'Maiden's Blush'."

complete yet always harmonious space. The paths meandered in different directions as certain roses outgrew their bounds; a gazebo in the center of the garden became a special place for drinking in the fragrance of roses on all sides. At various times, she added a reflecting pond, handcrafted benches, and small support structures, often expressing her delightful sense of humor through whimsical accessories and serendipitous touches.

Her 25 Alba varieties, including all the usual ones and those that are not often seen, make up the core of her collection of 350 cold-hardy bushes. While most Albas usually grow taller than their Damask parent, Gerry has examples of their versatile range from the most compact 'Jeanne d'Arc', which stays close to 4 feet, through the middle range of 'Belle Amour', which usually hits 5 to 6 feet, and the tallest in her garden—and her favorite—'Blush Hip', which usually rises to 7 feet. Recently, Gerry added a few of the new Hybrid Alba shrubs in the Blush series developed in Germany by Rolf Sievers. These Albas crossed with *kordesii* roses are old fashioned in appearance, strongly fragrant, and as hardy as both of their parents.

Among the most beautiful in Gerry's collection of twenty-five varieties of Rugosa roses are the long hedges of twenty-five 'Jens Munk' shrubs, whose beautiful lavender-pink blooms open repeatedly to show their luminous golden centers. Its luxuriant green foliage is a bonus in the garden, and although the orange-red hips are more sparse than on other Kordes roses in the garden, they do help in bringing birds into the garden for fall feasting.

As casual about garden planning as she is about the other aspects of horticulture, Gerry just digs a hole for a new rose bush or a new native perennial from the northern plains. When the chokecherry trees (*Prunus virginiana*) and the European bird cherries (*Prunus padus*) cast too much shade on the roses, she trims back the trees rather than moving the roses. "But to be safe, I also start another bush in a different part of the garden just to make sure I will always have at least one. I never really dig something up and move it. I just take a cutting and start over." The garden, a testimonial for her passionate love of roses, represents a persistence and skill that are rare even among rose growers. ❉

OPPOSITE A bouquet of Gerry Krueger's Albas, one of the oldest classes of the old garden roses, features what must be the whitest among the white Albas, 'Alba Maxima', in the center of the bouquet. 'Madame Legras de St. Germain' is another slightly creamier white, and the pinks include 'Maiden's Blush','Königin von Dänemark', and 'Blush Hip'.

PRECEDING PAGE Nestled beneath a soft green willow tree is a trio of pastels: 'Ester', a Gallica; 'Blush Hip', a favorite; and lavender *Salvia*.

LEFT Shrubs of 'Jens Monk', one of the "tough roses," grow beautifully in Gerry's 3-acre garden next to a native wildlife preserve. The fragrant, medium-pink blossoms—often with a streak of white—cover the shrub from spring through late summer. Its Rugosa background makes it hardy and disease resistant, and offers the dense mid-green foliage that makes 'Jens Munk' a perfect landscape shrub for regions where temperatures dip to −20 degrees.

STRUCTURING NATURE

FEW GARDENS BETTER REVEAL MAN'S HARMONIOUS RELATIONSHIP WITH NATURE THAN THAT OF THE NEELY GARDEN IN SEATTLE, WASHINGTON. ROBERT CHITTOCK, A SEATTLE-BASED LANDSCAPE ARCHITECT, ALSO WORKS IN HARMONY WITH HIS MANY CLIENTS AND PARTICULARLY

with Diana Neely, his client for the past twenty-five years. Chittock says, "Even after the garden was laid out, I continued to consult as needed." Although the Pacific Northwest's abundant rainfall and temperate winters make for ideal gardening conditions, Diana Neely's garden would not be so remarkable if it were not for her high standards of upkeep.

The 2½ acres that Michael and Diana Neely bought in 1969 had a tennis court in a front lawn that stretches to the banks of Lake Washington. Diana Neely and Bob Chittock knew that the magnificent view of the lake and of Mt. Rainier in the distance should not be interrupted. Removing the tennis court, redesigning the terrace to become a more attractive viewing spot, and regrading the lawn into a "breathing space," as the English landscape designers refer to their vast parklike lawns, were the first stage of the ongoing landscape project that continues to evolve fifteen years later.

Five elegant 'Sea Foam' tree roses in terra-cotta pots on a curving brick band border the parking court at the entrance and set the tone of structured harmony and quiet order with their dark green, disease-resistant foliage and profusion of creamy white blossoms.

The Neely formal garden has also been called the boxwood garden, the white garden, but, most appropriately, a garden for all seasons. The Japanese maple, dogwoods, Mt. Fuji cherries, fothergilla, and the enkianthus are as spectacular in the fall as they are in the spring. In winter, the stylized structure of the layout is made dramatically clear as boxwood beds and burlap-wrapped standard 'Iceberg' roses are outlined in whiteness and the branches of towering cedars are blanketed with snow.

By 1982, when the formal garden was begun, Diana Neely was well on her way to becoming a seriously respected plantswoman. She had visited the gardens of England and France, had learned a great deal from her mentor

Bob Chittock, and had devoted herself intensively to the study of horticulture, particularly of roses and shrubs that grow well in the Pacific Northwest. Like Vita Sackville-West's Sissinghurst, the English prototype of the white garden, the essentially white Neely garden admits touches of color in early spring and is enormously rich in plants despite its small size. Likewise, in the 60 by 80-foot Neely garden room there is an astonishing luxuriance of shrubs, trees, and unusual bedding plants. Even before the roses are in bloom, an undercurrent of white flowers begins with tulips, then lilies of the valley and pansies appear among the grays and silvers of artemisias, lavenders, lamb's ears, and lamiums. Early spring also brings out the white blooms of the star magnolias (*Magnolia stellata*). Both the columnar weeping gray pear trees (*Pyrus salicifolia* 'Pendula') and 'Iceberg' rose trees contribute to the formal structure. Even when the roses are not in bloom, they offer harmonious, scaled-down echoes

PRECEDING PAGE A collection of some of the white roses grown in Diana Neely's Seattle garden. From left to right, 'Iceberg'; 'Madame Hardy', with its distinctive green eye; 'Rosa rugosa Alba'; 'Sericea Pteracantha', known for blood-red thorns as beautiful as its blossoms; and a cluster of 'Rambling Rector', which climbs 25 feet into a cedar.

RIGHT The dependable repeat blooms and dark green foliage of standard 'Iceberg' roses maintain a consistent formal note while the underplantings change from season to season.

BELOW White with a blush of pink, 'Sea Foam' standards—grown in pots and underplanted with white petunias, Helichrysum, and trailing vinca—outline the curve of the driveway.

FOLLOWING PAGES Sensuous harmonies are structured in a geometric setting.

of the erect towering poplars in the background.

As the garden moves into summer and the roses begin their repeat-bloom flushes, white-flowering perennials fill in the underplantings—more than 300 varieties have been in the garden at a time, including cranesbill (*Geranium sanguineum* 'Album'), mouse plant (*Arisarum proboscideum*), bleeding heart (*Dicentra spectabilis* 'Alba'), violets, nicotiana, candelabra primulas, *Astrantia major*, columbine (variety 'Biedermeir'), native shooting stars (*Dodecatheon meadia* 'Album'), and almost always one of two kinds of phlox, including 'Admiral' and the taller, late-blooming 'Mt. Fuji'.

Although the garden has an English heritage, it is definitely a Pacific Northwestern creation. Many trees and plants such as western red cedar (*Thuja plicata*), *Sequoia sempervirens,* Oregon grape (*Mahonia aquifolium*), and *Oxalis oregana* are native. Other plants such as the umbrella plant (*Peltiphyllum peltatum*) and certain varieties of rhododendrons and azaleas have naturalized.

Native to Japan yet frequently grown in the Seattle area are stands of Japanese iris, fuki (*Petasites japonicus*), and *Enkianthus campanulatus*, all chosen for their unusual foliage and structure.

Bob Chittock remarks that "in English formal gardens the walkways are as important as the fields of plants." The Neely garden brick walkways, laid in a pleasing herringbone design, carry the line of sight straight through the garden on multiple axes and emphasize the strong architectural framework.

Adding to the formality at the center of the garden is a small pool filled with water lilies.

But it is the breathtakingly beautiful trees, the towering deodara (*Cedrus deodara*) and western red cedars, the hemlocks and the poplars that give this garden a sense of place. When Chittock began to work on the formal garden, these were already an important part of the landscape, along with the 1920s loggia, which has been completely rebuilt, and the seventy-year-old Concord grape vines. Collections of cherry trees, dogwoods, rhododendrons, camellias, and eleven varieties of magnolia have also been added.

While the informal planting within the formal boxwood parterres is rich and varied, there is a knowledgeable restraint in the choice of material. Diana has shown even greater restraint in her minimal use of roses in the formal area. She has kept her colorful roses at bay in the back garden, where the rambunctious Ramblers and Shrub roses can clamber into the trees or tumble over hydrangeas with a freedom not permitted in the formal garden room. In the back garden, her favorite Species, old garden, and Shrub roses join colorful Hybrid Teas that have no place in other parts of the garden.

The pruning, sculpting, and shaping of the vertically trained 'Iceberg' and 'Sea Foam' tree roses dramatically echoes nature's own geometry and offers, at various levels, a harmonious interplay with the strong verticality of the garden's natural bones. ❈

SEA FOAM

Shrub

Alain Meilland, the French hybridizer from the distinguished house of Meilland, paid the ultimate compliment to the American Ernest Schwartz, who produced 'Sea Foam': he grew two of his tree roses at the Meilland home in France. Meilland had high praise when Conard-Pyle introduced this versatile modern Shrub rose in 1964, acclaiming it as a "yet to be appreciated genetic breakthrough . . . It is so much more than a garden rose. It belongs most anywhere in the landscape."

'Sea Foam', with its mounds of white blossoms in sharp contrast to its dark green small-leafed, holly-like foliage, is very much appreciated today. It is used as a remarkably beautiful ground cover, as a pillar or climber whose arching canes sometimes reach 6 or 7 feet, as a graceful shrub weeping over a terrace wall, or even as an attractive broad low hedge. Diana Neely has grafted 'Sea Foam' as a tree rose with a curving band of five 36-inch-tall specimens. Placed in large terra-cotta pots, the 'Sea Foam' tree roses make a dramatic entrance to her Seattle garden.

'Sea Foam' blooms are usually pure white, but in cold or damp weather the full-blown roses are often a blushing pink.

Although described as extremely hardy to cold and wind, 'Sea Foam' standards are somewhat difficult to find through mail order, since tree roses in general are travel sensitive.

ALTHOUGH THE GARDEN has an English heritage, it is definitely a Pacific Northwestern creation. Many trees and plants such as western red cedar, *Sequoia sempervirens,* Oregon grape, and *Oxalis oregana* are native.

BLOOMS *on a* WINDY ISLE

FROM EVERY VANTAGE POINT IN THE 2½-ACRE GARDEN OF TINA AND BRUCE WEAKLY ON WHIDBEY ISLAND, WASHINGTON, ONE IS VERY MUCH AWARE OF BEING IN THE FAR REACHES OF THE PACIFIC NORTHWEST. PERHAPS IT IS BECAUSE ONE SEES FROM EVERY VIEW THE TOWERING

green belt of magnificent native Douglas fir (*Pseudotsuga menziesii*), moisture-loving alders (*Alnus oregona*), willows, and ocean spray (*Holodiscus discolor*), a native shrub that reaches up to 20 feet beyond the confines of the Weakly property. The evergreen trees offer a protective barrier from the wind and form a rich light-filtering backdrop for their garden. Although the Puget Sound is not within their garden view, a clean freshness in the air is a reminder that this is an island garden.

The modest three-bedroom house that the Weaklys built in 1986 sits in the middle of their 5-acre property, completely surrounded by the wilds of nature and their splendid collection of roses. A 330-foot-long driveway that runs between a forest on one side and open grassland meadow on the other is lined on both sides with Rugosa roses, many grown from seed by Tina Weakly.

Frequent winds that blow across the 40-mile-long Whidbey Island necessitate careful pruning of the roses in March to protect the long canes from being whipped off the numerous rose-covered arches. For further protection from the wind, Tina and Bruce also planted a double hedge of English laurel (*Prunus laurocerasus*) and 40-foot (and still growing) columnar poplars (*Populus nigra* 'Italica') along the width of their property, making an attractive screen from the road. In addition, the poplars silhouetted against the sky add to their view from the garden.

"Gardening is our life," says Tina, whose husband, Bruce, turned his hobby of metal- and woodworking into creating the well-designed bones of the garden: the edging of wood around the irregularly shaped beds, the more than twenty arbors, and the latest addition of finial-topped tripods scattered throughout the garden for the support of some of their profusely blooming climbers. In addition, Bruce's metal sculptures—glimpsed in the thicket of the woods or spotted as discreet adornments among the roses and their companions, or sometimes even atop a rose-covered arch—are all indications of Bruce's

appreciation of his wife's lifelong passion for gardening.

The Weakly roses numbering more than 700 have been grouped together in various beds around the house and are separated by grassy paths that meander from one section to another, often beneath arches that engulf the visitor with fragrance. Color often gives a specific bed its name: the white garden, the purple, pink, and lavender bed; or the orange and yellow "hot bed." Where possible, roses of different classes are mixed with companion plants of the same height, such as the seventeen different varieties of buddleia or the climbing sweet peas against the rose-covered arches. Sometimes a particular combination such as the soft blue clumps around the English rose 'Constance Spry' shows how pleasing an arrangement can be, simply around one rose. Climbers such as Hybrid Musks, Ramblers, and Large-flowered Climbers form the core of this collection. The Hybrid Musks alone number more than seventy varieties. Tina has often allowed

ROSA GLAUCA

Species

The European Species *Rosa glauca* (formerly *R. rubrifolia*) is often appreciated more for its foliage than its blossoms. As both its names suggest, the leaves of this European native are gray-green with a distinct mauve-purple sheen.

R. glauca mixes well in the perennial bed, its lovely soft foliage and ruby stems enhancing almost any neighboring plant. As a specimen shrub, *R. glauca* can stand alone, as its clusters of bright mahogany-red hips add color to the fall garden. It is used successfully as a hedge, especially when pruned regularly to encourage density, since its natural tendency is to be an open shrub. *R. glauca*'s tolerance of shade makes it particularly useful to landscape architects. Its thorns are minimal when compared with some of its sister Species roses. Tina Weakly in her Whidbey Island garden mixes the unthreatening *R. glauca* with other more modern roses chosen for their compatible color.

Some describe the blooms of *R. glauca* as insignificant, but upon closer examination, clusters of the 1½-inch starlike flowers are quite beautiful: five clear pink petals set off a white center and clear yellow stamens. Particularly when the foliage is used along with the blossoms, *R. glauca* offers unique possibilities for the discerning flower arranger.

them to intertwine with each other or with other rose-enhancing vines, such as clematis and honeysuckle.

Rhododendrons, Himalayan poppies (*Meconopsis betonicifolia*), primroses, and hostas all love the temperate, moist climate of Whidbey Island, which only occasionally dips below freezing in January and is rarely hot in summer. In fact, the climate of Whidbey is most often compared to another island famous for its gardens and as home to some of the world's most famous rose growers, England. But it takes more than the right climate to grow good roses the way Tina Weakly does.

The health of her roses is a priority, so Tina has become a selector as well as a collector. "The once-blooming old garden roses do not grow particularly well in this garden. They tend to get mildew after blooming," says Tina, "and Hybrid Teas are my least favorite. I grow roses for their beauty in the garden, but usually not for rose shows. We grow them for the pleasure of the numerous visitors who come when the garden is open to the public from May through September."

In strolling through the Weakly garden one might see in one bed a collection of Miniature roses intermixed with pansies and alyssum or, in other beds, foxglove, snapdragons, and alstroemeria that bring color at just the right height next to the occasional Floribunda or delicately nodding China and Tea

roses. Dianthus crowds in next to everything and the 7-foot-tall variegated *Buddleia davidii* 'Harlequin' bushes are ideal companions for the taller English roses. Fluffs of gypsophila and feathery artemisias bring different textures to the white garden.

Tina has cleverly brought the Pacific Northwest into the garden by allowing Ramblers, such as 'Paul's Himalayan Musk Rambler' and the climbing species 'Kiftsgate', to grow into the redwoods, willows, and spruce. Their dark, evergreen branches make a perfect foil for the roses when in bloom and, afterward, they fade into the green branches until the roses bloom again. And the buds of 'Lemon Light', a gracefully arching Rambler, lighten up the Ponderosa Redwood.

Tina's unique collection of twenty-six Species roses includes *R. californica* and *R. setigera,* both native American species that usually bloom later than their European cousins, *R. eglanteria* and *R. pimpinellifolia,* also known respectively as the Sweetbriar and Scotch briar roses. The 'Burnet Rose' (*R. spinosissima*) produces round black hips after the white blossoms have gone by in late June. Occasionally Tina mixes a Species rose with other more modern varieties, such as the beautiful single-flowered blood red *R. moyesii* hybrid that holds its own in the "hot garden" along with the modern roses in the red, yellow, orange, and bicolored range.

PRECEDING PAGE The Weaklys' garden boasts more than 700 roses, grouped loosely around the house with perennials and annuals.

ABOVE Grown as a 10-foot climber on Whidbey Island, 'English Elegance', the buff-colored blooms of the David Austin shrub, are spectacular in size.

LEFT Old Garden Roses are mixed with modern roses, including two climbing Floribundas: 'Dancing Doll' in the background and 'China Doll', a pink Polyantha that makes an excellent ground cover.

ALTHOUGH THE PUGET SOUND is not within their garden view, a clean freshness in the air is a reminder that this is an island garden.

The thorniest of the Species rose collection are not mixed into the modern Shrub bed or into the ground-cover bed, where weeding would be a painful chore. Instead, these are with others in the Species collection appropriately placed at the edge of the woodland garden, where they will be able to arch and sprawl or creep much as they do in the former wilds of North America, China, Asia, or on the slopes of the Pyrenees in Europe where they were originally found. As this fairly young garden has evolved Tina has linked the old and the new roses into a continuous, homogeneous flow that lasts from May through September. It is often her favorite blowsy Hybrid Musks that pair the new yet old-fashioned-looking David Austin English roses (fifty in all) with some of the Species roses—the oldest of all.

By far the best known in the Species class are *R. banksiae banksiae* and its yellow multiclustered cousin, *R. banksiae lutea,* which are grown in only the most protected sites on Whidbey Island but which in other more protected and warmer parts of the country grow rampantly and usually mark the first blooming roses of spring. On the other hand, Tina grows another favorite Species rose that is usually identified with warmer parts of the country, the gorgeous large white-flowered *R. laevigata* (Cherokee rose), whose glossy light green foliage is disease free. Though it comes from China, it was naturalized in the South and has become the state flower of Georgia.

Tina Weakly achieves a rich variety of effects by juxtaposing the cultivated and the wild, the structured and the unstructured, the monumental and the diminutive, the massive and the dainty, all the while establishing a balance between the tradition of a very well-groomed and harmoniously designed rose garden and an inventive reliance on indigenous flora. In this respect, Tina echoes the attitudes and practices of so many creative American gardeners who, like her, have loosened our traditional links with the European past through various design elements and horticultural opportunities drawn from the American setting. ✳

LEFT The vibrant oranges of 'Warm Welcome', a climbing Miniature, and 'Fragrant Cloud' are mixed with the orange and yellow blends of 'Trumpeter', 'Hiroshima's Children', and 'Playboy' in this lively section of the Weakly garden.

FOLLOWING PAGE Among the Hybrid Musks are, in the upper-right corner, the heavily petaled, dark carmine-rose-colored blooms of the Polyantha 'Excellenz von Schubert', which are unique among the single blooms of 'Moonlight', 'Belinda', 'Cornelia', and 'Ballerina'.

A BEAUTIFUL
ROSE GARDEN GUIDE

GROWING TIPS *from the* GARDENERS

As anyone who has ever tried to nurture a rose bush knows, much of growing beautiful roses is a trial-and-error process. For each individual garden, so many variables come into play—from soil type and amount of shade to temperature extremes and average annual rainfall—that the only way a rose gardener can be assured of success is to learn from past triumphs and failures. Common sense and the power of observation are the best tools a gardener can have.

In my own southern California garden, I've learned that my roses benefit from a biannual banquet of nutrient-rich food; for each rose bush I mix in a wheelbarrow 2 gallons each of forest humus and compost or oakleaf mold; 1 cup each of chicken manure, alfalfa meal, fish meal, and kelp; 1/2 cup epsom salts (for encouraging new canes); and 5 ounces Osmacote. I feed this mixture to my bushes every March and September, and have been rewarded with healthy canes, lush foliage, and an abundance of blossoms.

Below is a selection of the favorite methods and ideas developed by gardeners featured in this book. Although some of the suggestions may not work in your USDA zone, many can be adjusted to meet your individual needs, and all will inspire you to develop your own beautiful American rose garden.

ENSURING REPEAT BLOOMS

Mike Lowe
Nashua, New Hampshire
Pages 16–23

The most important factor in ensuring repeat bloom for repeat-blooming varieties is an abundance of *water*. And winter protection is important in New Hampshire and other cold zones. I put a large mound of earth around the crown or a Styrofoam "rose cone," but not both, beginning after the first year of planting.

PLANTING NEW BUSHES

Dieter Schmidt
Nantucket, Massachusetts
Pages 24–27

When digging a hole for a new rose bush, I always follow the advice of rosarian Rayford Reddell. First, I make it a big hole: 2 feet wide by 18 inches deep. Then I put aside half the removed soil, and mix in a wheelbarrow the other half with some new packaged soil and equal parts aged chicken manure and compost or peat moss or other organic material including 1 cup bone meal and 1 cup superphosphate. Put half of this mixture into the hole, creating a little hill in the hole. Place the rose bush on top of this hill, spreading the roots so that they drape down the sides. Then fill the hole with water and, when well drained, add the rest of the soil-enriched mixture and pat down with your hands—not with your feet. Finally, I make sure the rose is ground level and not too low, as it will sink anyway with time.

THE BASICS OF ROSE GROWING

David Dawn
Long Island, New York
Pages 28–35

Everyone is afraid to raise roses. They shouldn't be, because it is so easy, as long as you have five to six hours of sunshine a day, preferably facing east, and, most importantly, good drainage. During the summer months, we have to spray once a week. You can't have a garden like ours without it.

ROSE CARE IN FLORIDA

Jody Lowe
Palm Beach, Florida
Pages 36–41

Here roses thrive as long as they're on Fortuniana rootstock. Every two weeks we put on a balanced fertilizer, and twice a year we mulch with cow manure. Roses grow fast down here in Palm Beach, because of the fertilizing, humidity, and sunshine, so they have to be pruned back severely. There is no dormancy period for them, but the growth does slow down in winter. Our biggest problem is blackspot, and to combat it I use a spray with copper in it.

CONTROLLING INSECT AND FUNGAL DAMAGE

Ann-Mari Horkan
Loudon County, Virginia
Pages 47–53

In recent years I have found the organic product Rose Defense made by Green Light from oil of the neem tree to be the most ecologically safe remedy for controlling spider mites, aphids, white-flies, and fungus diseases such as rust and powdery mildew. Reluctantly, if leaf borers suddenly arrive, I make an immediate attack with Orthene or even the stronger Avid to completely eradicate the insect problem. Spraying, particularly in the heat, must be done carefully to avoid leaf-spotting, which is frowned upon by the flower show judges, as are any signs of foliage damage. When blackspot or leafspot finds its way to Cleremont Farm, no rose variety is completely immune to this fungus. Again, Rose Defense is the organic product I use. If the fungus persists, Funginex is alternated with a spray-

ing of Daconil, neither of which is extremely toxic when directions are followed carefully.

COMBATING JAPANESE BEETLES

Charlotte Hundley
Heathsville, Virginia
Pages 54–59

I am thankful Japanese beetles wait to make their appearance until after the first blooming cycle in mid-June and disappear before the beautiful fall blooms. To help control them, I follow rosarian Stephen Scanniello's recommendation of a repeat application of Milky Spore Disease—the bacteria that attacks the grubs. I also recommend the use of predatory nematodes to destroy Japanese beetle grubs. You can also handpick the grubs from your bushes and kill them by dropping them in a can of bleach water. A fine spray of Sevin just over the blooms will also kill these pests.

A GARDENER'S DISCIPLINE

Mary Hart Orr
Greensboro, North Carolina
Pages 60-63

All one needs to grow good roses is patience, because it takes at least two years to really see how a rose will do in your area, and courage, because you may have to pull the bush out if it is not successful or if you decide it was a mistake to have planted it in that location.

SANDY SOIL CONSIDERATIONS

Ruth Knopf
Coastal South Carolina
Pages 62–69

In my upstate garden, I fertilized only once a year, and I did not use high nitrogen chemical fertilizers. Roses treated this way build up strong growth over time, and are more disease and insect resistant. In my coastal garden with such sandy soil, fertilizing more often is necessary. I also find that with sandy soil PVC pipe used in the rose beds with a hole drilled at each bush works well and is economical. Concealing the piping with landscape fabric or black plastic and then covering it with a heavy mulch conserves moisture during our very hot summers.

ALL-AROUND PROTECTION

Pat Henry
Northwestern South Carolina
Pages 70–73

I found out I can treat almost everything from the top of the bushes only. For thrips I use a 75 percent wettable powdered Orthene before the buds show color in May. They must be treated before the big blooming, but when necessary I spray a fungicide over the entire plant. Miticides must be directed to the underside of the leaves.

THE VIRTUES OF OLD GARDEN ROSES

Patsy and Jack Holden
Bayou Chenal, Louisiana
Pages 78–83

We do no spraying and just let the bugs have their share. All of our roses are Old Garden Roses and are used to very little care, so we fertilize only once in the spring and prune for the shape of the rose bush and the beauty of the garden.

KEEPING ROSES IN SCALE IN SMALL GARDENS

David Caton
Houston, Texas
Pages 84–87

I do very little feeding—just in the spring—and I restrain from watering to help keep the roses down. I like to go light on feeding, because it reduces the amount of watering I have to do in the summer, and at the same time it keeps things in scale in my small garden. The more you fertililze, the more you have to water. This works because I have mostly Old Garden Roses.

CHOOSING COLORS FOR THE ROSE GARDEN

Anne H. Bass
Fort Worth, Texas
Pages 88–93

Russell Page advised me to mix colors in my rose garden, the idea being that I could easily replace a damaged plant. I have also found this allows for experimentation, which is fortunate, as I cannot read an extensive rose catalog without being seduced by at least a dozen new plants. But mixing colors does not mean "anything goes." One must have a palette in mind. In my main garden, for example, there is a dominant blue tone (blue-pink, blue-red, etc.), and in a separate section we have used cream, buff, apricot, and yellow shades.

WINTERIZING ROSES

John Cotta
Ladue, Missouri
Pages 94–99

After the first freeze when the temperatures stay close to freezing for a few days, I cut the rose bushes back to about knee level. All the beds are then outlined with chicken wire and stakes are planted to support the sides. We use shredded leaves accumulated from the mower and shredded bark or other mulch, which is carefully filled in around the roses to almost the top of their chicken wire confines. In the spring, after the last chance of freezing, the chicken wire comes down, the leaf mulch is removed, and the roses can be cut back to remove any winter damage.

THE IMPORTANCE OF TIMING IN DISEASE CONTROL

Tom Carruth
Altadena, California
Pages 104–107

Timing helps in controlling regular mildew (powdery as opposed to downy), rust, and other fungal problems. After cleaning up all the old foliage, we use a dormant spray—a combination of copper, sulfur, and modern oils. Also, by not pruning too early, fungal diseases are combated. Powdery mildew loves succulent new growth so that in southern California it is best to prune later—not before January 15 inland and February 1 in the coastal areas. Good circulation helps reduce fungus problems as well.

THE ADVANTAGES OF SMALL PLASTIC BASINS AROUND ROSES

Charles Follette
Hollywood, California
Pages 108–113

Most people build and rebuild their basins around the roses in order to keep the water and fertilizer localized. I just build a permanent plastic basin around the perimeter of the rose (around 14 inches in diameter) that goes down 3 inches, allowing the fertilizer and the water to go directly to the roots without any runoff or waste. The basin also prevents the soil from covering the bud union, which can cause disease and decay. The air circulation is increased and the plant is kept clean and healthy.

ACCESSORIES AND STRUCTURES IN THE GARDEN

Pat McNamara
Pasadena, California
Pages 114–117

Aside from the plants themselves, gardens are made more interesting by the choice of materials in pathways and border outlines. Sculptures and other man-made accessories should enhance, not compete with, the serenity of the landscape. Structures such as arbors, pavillions, pergolas, and trellises not only provide different vertical elements, but are also a great way of lifting roses to a higher level.

DESIGNING WITH ROSES

Dan Kiley
Charlotte, Vermont
Pages 118–123

We are always dealing with the whole, not unrelated parts. People often jump to details too quickly, before the idea of the whole is established. Rose parterres work well in the Lears' garden because they are the appropriate scale in relation to the rest of the garden, and they are protected in the east and south exposures of the house/landscape structure. The rose garden must be an organic part of the whole landscape. As for colors, I prefer subtle, limited contrasts of color. A mass of one color, punctuated with one or two others, is much more effective than a blatant mix of many shades.

WATERING IN THE SOUTHWEST

Terri Campbell
Ojai, California
Pages 124–129

In our arid air climate of the Ojai Valley, there is a lot of transpiration, so we have to water more frequently. The only rainfall we are blessed with occurs during the winter months. Drip irrigation is the best solution for us. We monitor it with a computer since we are sure of having no rain from March to November. I water once a week for 50 minutes until the temperature reaches 80°F., then twice a week. In summer when it is very hot we do overhead watering once a week—mostly to wash off the roses. Heavy mulching—up to 8 inches—keeps moisture in the soil.

PREVENTING DOWNY MILDEW

Dan Bifano
Santa Barbara, California
Pages 130–135

If one uses a dormant spray with a copper or zinc base such as Subdue, Champ or Fore at pruning time in January, it will usually prevent the emergence of downy mildew in April and May, when the fungus is most prevalent in coastal California rose gardens like the Halsteds'. If the dormant spray has not been used at that time, I recommend a thorough drenching every week for three weeks with Daconil (always following label instructions carefully). By the time the weather warms up and the second flush of roses comes forth, the problem should have gone away.

INNOVATIVE PRUNING

Gregg Lowery
Sebastopol, California
Pages 136–141

Pruning roses to keep them healthy and shapely is easy. The simplest approach is to forget the traditional rules and to use your own common sense and powers of observation. I focus on thinning out the very old, twiggy, and congested wood, starting from the base and inside. Once I have done that, the healthy structure of each rose emerges. Then I have only to reduce the scale more or less by pruning back the remaining branches to strong, healthy growth buds. Each variety has a personality; some roses renew their main canes regularly from the base, while others keep their wood in a productive state for much longer. Observe such charateristic habits from year to year, and pruning becomes a pleasurable learning experience. Avoid at all costs the needlessly complex procedure of making pruning cuts on an angle; these cuts can leave larger wounds on rose canes, which will cost the plants more energy to heal over. To prune on this "correct" angle also takes more time than a simple straight cut perpendicular to the stem, which is easier for the gardener and better for the rose. Climbing and once-blooming roses are pruned just like other roses, but more lightly. Every few years they may be thinned more vigorously. Pruning robs all plants of stored energy which they would use to create new growth, yet it can effectively reduce disease by stripping out old foliage where fungi reside, and bringing air and light into the plant. Consider both when deciding how much to prune.

THE BENEFITS OF MULCHING

Danny Hills and Wayne Hughes
Portland, Oregon
Pages 146–149

When we lay out a new bed in the garden, we first mark off the area with garden hoses to get the general shape, and then we cover it with cardboard. We then put 4 inches of mulch over the entire area. The cardboard kills the grass and weeds underneath and attracts worms that eat the cardboard and dead grass. A year later the soil will be luscious. The bones of the garden—shrubs and roses—are planted immediately: punch 2-foot-square holes through the cardboard and amend the planting holes with more mulch, organic material, and compost. We then let it go for a year. By that time all the cardboard has broken down or been eaten by the wonderful worms and the soil is uniform. The shrubs have been given the time to get their feet into the soil, and the following spring we mulch primarily to suppress weeds and to retain moisture. We do not need to further mulch for winter protection in our area. In July and August, we cover any exposed soil with mulch to keep the weeds down and to keep the roots consistently moist and cool. This is almost more important for a beautiful garden than nutrients.

GROWING ROSES IN THE SEMI-SHADE

Gerry Krueger
Spokane, Washington
Pages 150–155

Although all roses prefer as much sun as possible, Albas are much more forgiving about partial shade than other varieties. All hardy Old Garden Roses will tolerate excessive abuse and neglect, which makes them a particular joy to casual gardeners. Here in the extreme hot and cold climate of Spokane, roses have got to be tough. Just stick the right roses in the ground and let them go.

ORGANIC FERTILIZING

Tina Weakly
Whidby Island, Washington
Pages 162–168

Our roses get a good start when first planted in a soil-enriched hole. After the first bloom we feed organically with the following: 2 parts alfalfa meal to 1 part each cottonseed meal, bone meal, blood meal, and kelp. We water this mixture in with diluted fish emulsion—in spring only—1 cup for a full size bush and smaller amounts accordingly. Through the spring and summer, I apply a little fish emulsion occasionally. After August 1, I never fertilize because it encourages new growth. We mulch in the fall with horse manure that is somewhat aged. I don't deadhead after the last of the season to encourage plants to go dormant. The roses we grow (Polyanthas, Hybrid Musks, Floribundas, and Shrubs) respond positively to this diet. But Hybrid Teas need a little more fertilizing, and more often, so I use Osmacote.

GARDEN PLANS *for* INSPIRATION

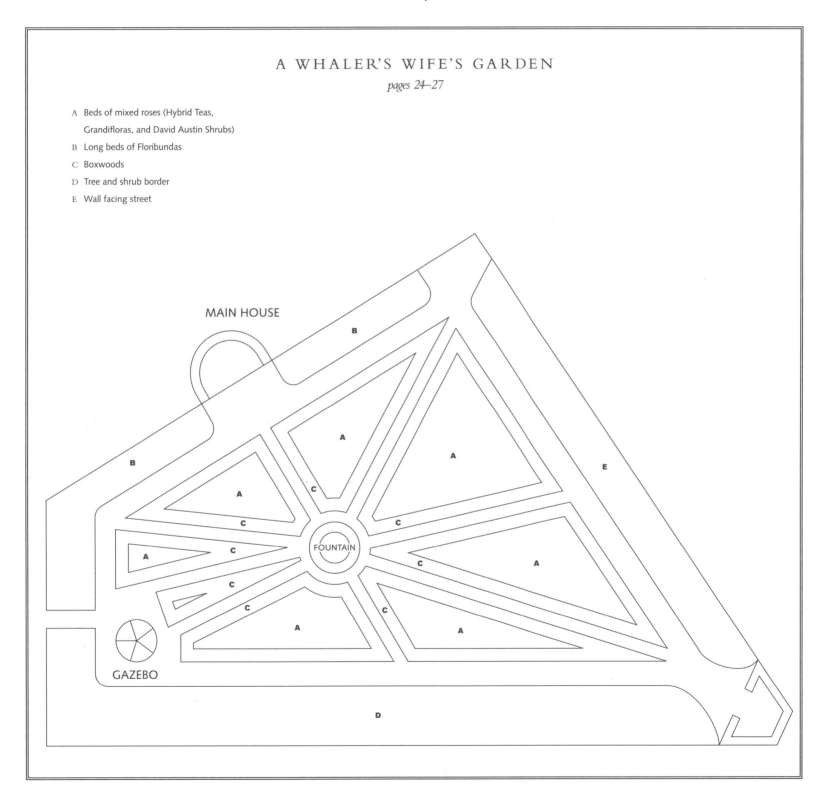

A WHALER'S WIFE'S GARDEN
pages 24–27

A Beds of mixed roses (Hybrid Teas,
   Grandifloras, and David Austin Shrubs)
B Long beds of Floribundas
C Boxwoods
D Tree and shrub border
E Wall facing street

MAIN HOUSE

B

B

A

A

A

C

C

C

A

C

FOUNTAIN

C

A

C

A

C

GAZEBO

C

A

A

D

E

OLD ROSES AT THE PLANTATION

pages 62–69

A Teas
B Noisettes
C Chinas and Teas
D Red Chinas
E *Rosa roxburghi*
F Climbers on pillars
G Grass
H Wide sand path
I Paths of brick originally made
   on the plantation

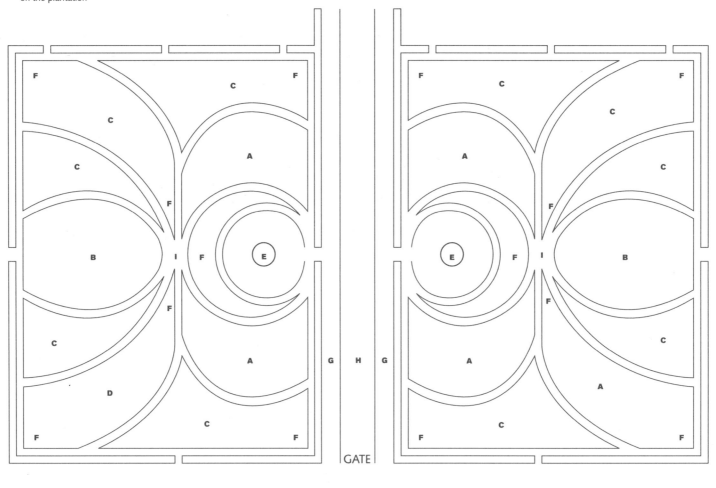

A REMEMBRANCE OF
THINGS PAST

pages 78–83

A Period annuals and perennials

B Sago palm

C Privet hedge

D 'Duchesse de Brabant'

E 'Louis Philippe'

F 'Malmaison'

G Moss roses

H Ruellia

I Chicksaw rose

J Honeysuckle

K Four o'clocks

L Lantana

M Cape Jasmine (gardenia)

N Banana shrub (*Magnolia fuscata*)

O Sweet olive

P Carolina jasmine

Q Fern

R Vegetables, herbs, and cutting flowers

S Muscadini grape arbor

T 'Lady Banksia'

U Mock orange

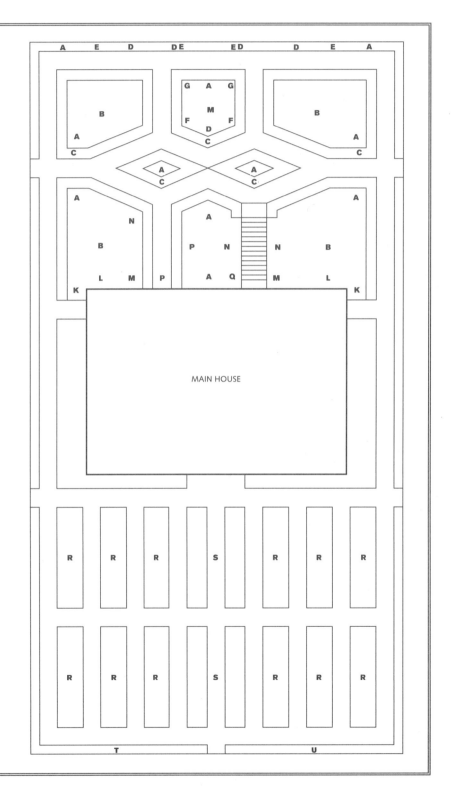

FORMALITY AND GRACE IN THE MIDWEST

pages 94–99

A   Pink 'Simplicity'
B   White 'Simplicity'
C   Red 'Simplicity'
D   'Iceberg'
E   'Bonica'
F   'Apricot Nectar'
G   'John F. Kennedy'
H   'French Lace'
I   'Brandy'

J   'Tropicana'
K   'Mr. Lincoln'
L   'White Lightning'
M   'Garden Party'
N   'Just Joey'
O   'Olympiad'
P   'Medallion'
Q   'Tiffany'
R   'Sheer Bliss'

HOUSE

POOL

HOLLYWOOD BEAUTIES
pages 108–113

A   Hybrid Teas

B   Floribundas

C   Climbers

D   Standards

E   Shrubs

PRESERVATION FOR THE FUTURE
pages 136–141

A   Old Europeans

B   Bourbons, Portlands,
      and Hybrid Perpetuals

C   Hybrid Teas and
      Floribundas

D   Modern Shrubs

E   Teas and Chinas

F   Repeat-blooming
      old roses

G   Old Hybrid Teas

H   Climbing roses

I   Species roses

J   Hybrid Musks

K   Single roses

L   Future mixed borders

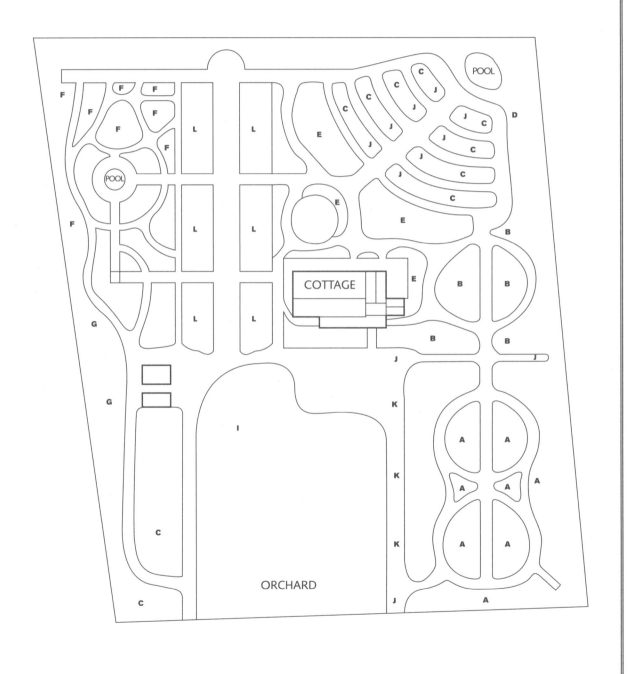

OREGON TURN-OF-THE-CENTURY CHARM

pages 146–149

A   Perennials: dahlias, peonies, and iris

B   Matching bed of perennials centered with
'Erfurt' rose

C   Garden gate covered with 'Dr. Van Fleet' rose

D   Perennial bed with the roses 'Bobbie James',
'Silver Moon', 'Dortmund', and 'Madame
Alfred Carrière'

E   Perennials, daylilies, and Hybrid Rugosas

F   Perennials with the roses 'Madame Hardy',
'Windchimes', and 'Moonlight'

G   Herbs

H   Lawn

I   Wild area

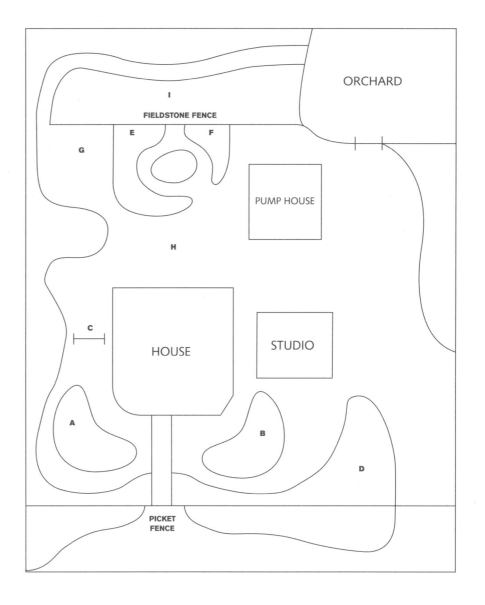

SOURCE LIST

Happily for American gardeners, North America has a bounty of nurseries, greenhouses, rootstock and seed companies, and gardens that grow and sell roses to the public. Most of the following places have catalogs or price lists and will send plants via mail-order. After each address, I have included some of the varieties in which the nursery specializes, and have cross-referenced each rose to their photograph and description in text.

Almost Heaven Antique Roses
229 Rickard Lane
Iron Station, NC 28080
(707) 732-4787
*Recommended source for 'Blush Noisette'
(see page 73), 'Ballerina' (see page 135)*

The Antique Rose Emporium
9300 Lueckemeyer Road
Brenham, TX 77833-6453
(409) 836-9051
*Recommended source for 'Blush Noisette' (see
page 73), 'Green Rose' (see page 67), 'Duchesse
de Brabant' (see page 81), 'Clotilde Soupert'
(see page 87), 'Autumn Damask' (see page
127), 'Ballerina' (see page 135), 'Baronne
Prévost' (see page 138)*

Arena Rose Company
P.O. Box 3096
Paso Robles, CA 93447
(805) 227-4094 or (602) 266-2223
*Recommended source for 'Autumn Damask'
(see page 127)*

Bay Laurel Nursery
2500 Camino Real
Atascadero, CA 93422
(805) 466-3406
*Recommended source for 'Tiffany' (see page
99), 'Scentimental' (see page 107)*

Bridges Roses
2734 Toney Road
Lawndale, NC 28090
(704) 538-9412
*Recommended source for 'Irresistible' (see
page 50)*

W. Atlee Burpee & Co.
300 Park Avenue
Warminster, PA 18991
(800) 888-1447
*Recommended source for 'Bonica'
(see page 112)*

Butner's Old Mill Nursery
806 South Belt Highway
St. Joseph, MO 64507
(816) 279-7434
*Recommended source for 'Tiffany' (see page
99), 'Just Joey' (see page 122)*

Carroll Gardens
444 East Main Street
Westminster, MD 21157
(503) 852-7135
*Recommended source for 'Rhonda' (see page
62), 'The Fairy' (see page 92), 'Just Joey' (see
page 122)*

Chamblee's Rose Nursery
10926 U.S. Hwy 69 North
Tyler, TX 75706-8742
(800) 256-7673
*Recommended source for 'Green Rose' (see page
67), 'Duchesse de Brabant' (see page 81),
'Clotilde Soupert' (see page 87), 'The Fairy'
(see page 92), 'Baronne Prévost' (see page 138)*

Donovan's Roses
P.O. Box 37800
Shreveport, LA 71133-7800
(318) 861-6693
*Recommended source for 'Tiffany' (see page
99), 'Scentimental' (see page 107)*

Edmunds' Roses
6235 S.W. Kahle Road
Wilsonville, OR 97070
(503) 682-1476
*Recommended source for 'Scentimental' (see
page 107), 'Just Joey' (see page 122)*

Forestfarm
990 Tetherow Road
Williams, OR 97544-9599
(541) 846-7269
*Recommended source for Rosa glauca
(see page 164)*

Garden Valley Ranch

498 Pepper Road

Petaluma, CA 94952

(707) 795-0919

Recommended source for 'Rhonda' (see page 62), 'Tiffany' (see page 99), 'Bonica' (see page 112)

Giles Ramblin' Roses

2968 State Road

710 Okeechobee, FL 34974

(941) 763-6611

Recommended source for 'Rhonda' (see page 62), 'Green Rose' (see page 67)

Greenmantle Nursery

3010 Ettersburg Road

Garberville, CA 95542

(707) 986-7504

Recommended source for 'Blush Noisette' (see page 73)

Hardy Roses for the North

Box 9

Danville, WA 99121

(250) 442-8842

Recommended source for 'Scentimental' (see page 107), 'Bonica' (see page 112), Rosa glauca (see page 164)

Heirloom Old Garden Roses

24062 Riverside Drive N.E.

St. Paul, OR 97137

(503) 538-1576

Recommended source for 'Canterbury' (see page 39), 'Green Rose' (see page 67), 'The Fairy' (see page 92), 'Just Joey' (see page 122), 'Autumn Damask' (see page 127), 'Ballerina' (see page 135), 'Bobbie James' (see page 148)

High Country Roses

P.O. Box 148

Jensen, UT 84035

(801) 789-5512

Recommended source for 'Linda Campbell' (see page 31), 'Autumn Damask' (see page 127), 'Bobbie James' (see page 148)

Historical Roses

1657 West Jackson Street

Painesville, OH 44077

(440) 357-7270

Recommended source for 'Maiden's Blush' (see page 152)

Hortico, Inc.

723 Robson Road, R.R. 1

Waterdown, Ontario

LOR 2H1, Canada

(905) 689-6984

Recommended source for 'Bobbie James' (see page 148)

Howerton Rose Nursery

1656 Weaversville Road

Allen Township

Northampton, PA 18067

(610) 262-5412

Recommended source for 'Tiffany' (see page 99)

Inter-State Nurseries

1800 Hamilton Road

Bloomington, IL 61704

(309) 663-9551

Recommended source for 'Tiffany' (see page 99)

Jackson & Perkins Co.

One Rose Lane

Medford, OR 97501-0702

(800) 292-4769

Recommended source for 'Ballerina' (see page 135)

J. W. Jung Seed Co.

335 South High Street

Randolph, WI 53957

(800) 247-5864

Recommended source for 'Scentimental' (see page 107), 'Baronne Prévost' (see page 138)

Justice Miniature Roses

5947 S.W. Kahle Road

Wilsonville, OR 97070-9727

(503) 682-2370

Recommended source for 'Irresistible' (see page 50) and other Miniatures

Sam Kedem Greenhouse and Nursery

12414 191st Street East

Hastings, MN 55033

(612) 437-7516

Recommended source for 'Irresistible' (see page 50), 'Bonica' (see page 112)

Limberlost Roses

7304 Forbes Avenue

Van Nuys, CA 91406-2737

(818) 901-7798

Recommended source for 'Blush Noisette' (see page 73)

Lowe's Own Root Roses
6 Sheffield Road
Nashua, NH 03062
(603) 888-2214
Recommended source for 'Oeillet Panachée' and other Mosses (see page 19), 'Blush Noisette' (see page 73), 'Green Rose' (see page 67), 'Maiden's Blush' (see page 152)

Martha S. Davies Antique Roses
1575 Palm Place South
Bartow, FL 33830
(941) 533-3073
Recommended source for 'Duchesse de Brabant' (see page 81)

Martin School Roses
10 S. Holland Sylvania Road
Toledo, OH 43615
(419) 866-4241
Recommended source for 'Baronne Prévost' (see page 138)

Mellinger's Inc.
2310 W. South Range Road
North Lilma, OH 44452
(330) 549-9861
Recommended source for 'Bonica' (see page 112)

Michael's Premier Roses
9759 Elder Creek Drive
Sacramento, CA 95829
(916) 369-7673
Recommended source for 'Irresistible' (see page 50), 'Green Rose' (see page 67)

Michigan Miniature Roses
45951 Hull Road
Belleville, MI 48111
(313) 699-6698
Recommended source for 'Irresistible' (see page 50) and other Miniatures

The Mini-Rose Garden
P.O. Box 203
Cross Hill, SC 29332
(864) 998-4331
Recommended source for 'Irresistible' (see page 50) and other Miniatures

Nor'East Miniature Roses, Inc.
58 Hammond Street
P.O.Box 307
Rowley, MA 01969
(978) 948-7964
Recommended source for 'Irresistible' (see page 50) and other Miniatures

Northland Rosarium
9405 S. Williams Lane
Spokane, WA 99224
(509) 448-4968
Recommended source for Rosa glauca (see page 164)

Oregon Miniature Roses, Inc.
8285 S.W. 185th Avenue
Beaverton, OR 97007-6712
(503) 649-4482
Recommended source for 'Irresistible' (see page 50) and other Miniatures

A Passion for Roses
P.O. Box 1050
Davis, CA 95617
(916) 753-6941
Recommended source for 'Tiffany' (see page 99)

Petaluma Rose Company
P.O. Box 750953
Petaluma, CA 94975
(707) 769-8862
Recommended source for 'Blastoff' (see page 59)

Pickering Nurseries, Inc.
670 Kingston Road
Pickering, Ontario
LIV 1A6, Canada
(905) 839-2111
Recommended source for 'Oeillet Panachée' and other Mosses (see page 19), 'Maiden's Blush' (page 152), Rosa glauca (page 164)

Regan Nursery
4268 Decoto Rod
Fremont, CA 94555
(510) 797-3222
Recommended source for 'Canterbury' (see page 39), 'Blastoff' (see page 59), 'Rhonda' (see page 62), 'Blush Noisette' (see page 73), 'Clotilde Soupert' (see page 87), 'Maiden's Blush' (page 152), 'Sea Foam' (page 159)

Rose Hill Garden
4955 Highway 9955 West
Ethel, LA 70730
(504) 634-3380
Recommended source for 'Clotilde Soupert' (see page 87), 'Ballerina' (see page 135)

The Roserie at Bayfields
P.O. Box R
Waldobro, ME 04572
(207) 832-6330
Recommended source for 'Ballerina' (see page 135), 'Maiden's Blush' (see page 152), Rosa glauca (see page 164)

Roses Unlimited
Route 1, Box 587
North Deerwood Drive
Laurens, SC 29360
(864) 682-7673
Recommended source for 'Rhonda' (see page 62), 'Blush Noisette' (see page 73), 'Green Rose' (see page 67), 'Duchesse de Brabant' (see page 81), 'Clotilde Soupert' (see page 87), 'Baronne Prévost' (see page 138)

Russian River Rose Company
1685 Magnolia Drive
Healdsburg, CA 95448
(707) 433-7455
Recommended for 'Blastoff' (page 59)

Sequoia Nursery
Moore Miniature Roses
2519 East Noble Avenue
Visalia, CA 93292
(209) 732-0190
Recommended source for 'Linda Campbell' (see page 31), 'Green Rose' (see page 67), 'Irresistible' (page 50) and other Miniatures

Spring Valley Roses
P.O. Box 7
Spring Valley, WI 54767
(715) 778-4481
Recommended source for Rosa glauca (see page 164)

Stanek's
2929 E 27th Avenue
Spokane, WA 99223
(509) 535-2939
Recommended source for 'Blastoff' (see page 59)

Sweet Briar Farm
14825 You Win Court
Grass Valley, CA 95945
(530) 477-7346
Recommended source for 'Bobbie James' (see page 148)

Taylor Roses
P.O. Box 677
Fairhope, AL 36533-0677
Recommended source for 'Irresistible' (see page 50) and other Miniatures

Teas Nursery Co., Inc.
4400 Bellaire Boulevard
Bellaire, TX 77401-4398
(713) 664-4400
Recommended source for 'Blush Noisette' (see page 73), 'Duchesse de Brabant' (see page 81), 'Clotilde Soupert' (see page 87), 'The Fairy' (see page 92)

Tiny Petals Nursery
489 Minot Avenue
Chula Vista, CA 91910-4833
(619) 422-0385
Recommended source for 'Irresistible' (see page 50) and other Miniatures

Vintage Gardens
2833 Gravenstein Hwy. South
Sebastapol, CA 95472
(707) 829-2035
Recommended source for 'Oeillet Panachée' and other Mosses (see page 19), 'Canterbury' (see page 39), 'Rhonda' (see page 62), 'Blush Noisette' (see page 73), 'Green Rose' (see page 67), 'Duchesse de Brabant' (see page 81), 'Clotilde Soupert' (see page 87), 'The Fairy' (see page 92), 'Autumn Damask' (see page 127), 'Ballerina' (see page 135), 'Baronne Prévost' (see page 138), 'Bobbie James' (see page 148), 'Maiden's Blush' (see page 152), Rosa glauca (see page 164)

Wayside Gardens
1 Garden Lane
Hodges, SC 29695-0001
(800) 845-1124
Recommended source for 'Linda Campbell' (see page 31), 'Rhonda' (see page 62), 'The Fairy' (see page 92), 'Tiffany' (see page 99)

White Flower Farm
P.O. Box 50
Litchfield, CT 06759
(800) 503-99624
Recommended source for 'Bonica' (see page 112)

Witherspoon Rose Culture
P.O. Box 52489
Durham, NC 27717
(919) 489-4446
Recommended source for 'Scentimental' (see page 107)

BIBLIOGRAPHY

American Rose Society. *Modern Roses 10: The Comprehensive List of Roses of Historical and Botanical Importance, Including All Modern International Rose Registrations.* Edited by Thomas Cairns. Shreveport, La.: The American Rose Society, 1993.

American Rose Society Committee on Judges, The. *Guidelines for Judging Roses: The Official American Rose Society Judges' Handbook, 1987 revisions.* Ed Griffith, Chairman. Shreveport, La.: The American Rose Society, 1987.

Austin, David. *David Austin's English Roses: Glorious New Roses for American Gardens.* Boston: Little Brown, 1993.

———. *Old Roses and English Roses.* London: Antique Collectors' Club, 1992.

———. *Shrub Roses and Climbing Roses.* London: Antique Collectors' Club, 1993.

———. *The Heritage of the Rose.* London: Antique Collectors' Club, 1988.

Beales, Peter. *Classic Roses.* New York: Holt, Rinehart and Winston, 1985.

———. *Visions of Roses.* Boston: Little Brown and Company, 1996.

———. *Roses: The Illustrated Encyclopedia and Grower's Handbook of Species Roses, Old Roses, Modern Roses, Shrub Roses and Climbers.* New York: Henry Holt & Co., 1992.

Christopher, Thomas. *In Search of Lost Roses.* New York: Avon Books, 1989.

Dickerson, Brent C. *The Old Rose Advisor.* Portland, Ore.: Timber Press, Inc., 1992.

Dobson, Beverly R., and Peter Schneider. *Combined Rose List 1998.* P.O. Box 677, Mantua, Ohio 44255.

Druitt, Liz. *The Organic Rose Garden.* Dallas: Taylor Press, 1991.

Druitt, Liz, and G. Michael Shoup. *Landscaping with Antique Roses.* Newtown, Conn.: The Tauton Press, 1992.

Edwards, Gordon. *Wild and Old Garden Roses.* Palo Alto, Calif.: Sweetbrier Press, 1975.

Ellwanger, H. B. *The Rose.* New York: Dodd, Mead & Company, 1893.

Ellwanger & Barry Catalogs for Mount Hope Nurseries. (5th and 6th editions). Rochester, New York: Ellwanger & Barry, 1900–1904.

Fearnley-Whittingstall, Jane. *Rose Gardens.* New York: Henry Holt & Co., 1989.

Gibson, Michael. *Fifty Favourite Roses: A Choice Selection for Every Gardener.* London: Cassell, 1995.

Griffiths, Trevor. *The Book of Old Roses.* London: Michael Joseph Limited, 1984.

Harkness, Jack. *The Makers of Heavenly Roses.* London: J. M. Dent & Sons Ltd., 1978.

Heard, Virginia Scott. *Nantucket Gardens and Houses.* Boston: Little Brown and Company, 1990.

Hole, S. Reynolds. *A Book About Roses: How to Grow and Show Them.* London: Edward Arnold, 1910.

Jekyll, Gertrude. *Roses for English Gardens.* London: Antique Collectors' Club, 1990.

Keays, Mrs. Frederick Love. *Old Roses.* New York: The MacMillan Company, 1935.

Lacy, Allen. *The Glory of Roses.* New York: Stewart, Tabori & Chang, 1990.

New York Botanical Garden, The. *Reliable Roses.* New York: Clarkson Potter, 1997.

Parsons, Samuel B. Parsons. *On the Rose: A Treatise on the Propagation, Culture, and History of the Rose.* New York: Orange Judd Company, 1891.

Page, Russell. *The Education of a Gardener.* New York: Random House, 1962.

Phillips, Rober, and Martyn Rix. *The Quest for the Rose: The Most Highly Illustrated Historical Guide to Roses.* New York: Random House, 1993.

————. *The Random House Guide to Roses,* New York: Random House, Inc. 1988.

Reddell, Rayford Clayton. *Growing Good Roses.* New York: Harper & Row, 1988.

————. *The Rose Bible.* New York: Harmony Books, 1994.

————. *A Year in the Life of a Rose.* New York: Harmony Books, 1996.

Scaniello, Stephen, and Tania Bayard. *Roses of America: The Brooklyn Botanic Garden's Guide to Our National Flower.* New York: Henry Holt & Co., 1990.

————. *A Year of Roses.* New York: Henry Holt and Company, 1997.

Shepherd, Roy E. *History of the Rose.* New York: The Macmillan Company, 1954.

Snyder, Leon C. *Gardening in the Upper Midwest.* Mineapolis: Univerity of Minnesota Press, 1978.

Thomas, Graham Stuart, et al. *A Garden of Roses.* Topsfiled, Mass.: Salem House Publishers, 1987.

————. *The Graham Stuart Thomas Rose Book.* Portland, Ore.: Saga Press/Timber Press, Inc., 1994.

Vaughn, Thomas, and Virginia Guest Ferriday, eds. *Space, Style & Structure: Building in Northwest America.* Portland, Ore.: Oregon Historical Society, 1974.

Verrier, Suzanne. *Rosa Gallica.* Deer Park, Wis.: Capability's Books, 1996.

————. *Rosa Rugosa.* Deer Park, Wis.: Capability's Books, 1995.

Zuzek, Kathy, Marcia Richards, Steve McNamara, Harold Pellett. *Roses for the North: Performance of Shrub and Old Garden Roses at the Minnesota Landscape Arboretum.* St. Paul, Minn.: Minnesota Agricultural Experiment Station, University of Minnesota, 1995.

INDEX

clematis, **148**

Clements, Louise, 148

'Climbing China Doll', 62, **62**

climbing roses, **18**, 22, **26**, 28, **30**, 31, **33**, 61–62, 64, 87, **87**, **110**, 112, **126**, 135, 146, 162, 164. *See also* Ramblers

'Clio', **139**

'Clotilde Soupert', 87, **87**

'Clytemnestra', 135

'Cocktail', **126**

'Color Magic', **135**

columbine, 159

companion plants
    annuals and perennials, 87, **92**, 104, 114, 117, 125, **126**, 127, 130, **135**, **139**, 147, **148**, 156, **158**, 159, **161**, 164, **167**
    grasses and sedges, 19, **87**, **102**, 104, 107, **107**, 125, **126**
    succulents, 87, **87**, **102**, 107, **107**
    trees and shrubs, **18**, 22, 25, **26**, 36, **39**, **50**, 54, **56**, 61, 71, **76**, 79, **80**, 81, **91**, 92, 94, **102**, 117, 121, 125, **135**, 152, 156, 159, **161**, 162, 164
    vines, 81, 114, **126**, **148**

Conard-Pyle, 62, 159

'Constance Spry', **33**, 162

coreopsis, **66**, **126**, 127

'Cornelia', **167**

Corydalis cashmeriana 'Blue Panda', 62

Cotta, John, 94–99, 172

'Country Dancer', 71

'Cramoisi Superieur', 64, 67

cranesbill, 114, 159

'Crépuscule', 64

Cupressus sempervirens (cypress), 92

Cycas revuluta (sago palm), 79

cypress, 92

D

'Dainty Bess', 112

Damask roses, **18**, 127, **127**, 152

'Dancing Doll', **165**

'Dapple Dawn', **148**

David Austin roses (English roses), **33**, 36–39, **39**, 49, **50**, 87, **91**, 162, **165**

Dawn, Helga and David, 28–35, 170

daylily, **59**

Dayton, Alan and Joanne, 36–41

delphinium, 147

deodara, 159

dianthus, **62**, 164

Dicentra spectabilis 'Alba' (bleeding heart), 159

'Dicky', 47

diseases, 27, 67, 135, 146, 171–174
    blackspot, 27, 171
    downy mildew, 135, 173
    leafspot, 171
    powdery mildew, 171, 172

'Distant Drums', 71

Dodecatheon meadia 'Album' (shooting star), 159

dogwood, 94, 156

'Dortmund', 28, 31, 146, 148, **148**

'Double Delight', 47, 92

'Dr. W. Van Fleet', 146

'Dublin Bay', **126**

'Ducher', 84

'Duchesse de Brabant', 81, **81**

'Duchess of Portland', 22

'Duet', 109, **135**

E

'Eden', **148**

'Elina', **33**, 54

'English Elegance', **165**

English laurel, 162

English roses. *See* David Austin roses

Enkianthus campanulatus, 156, 159

Erigeron karvinskianus (Santa Barbara daisy), 114

Erodium chrysanthemum (cranesbill), 114

Eschscholzia californica (California poppy), 130, **167**

'Ester', 152

eucalyptus, 125

'Europeana', **33**

European bird cherry, 152

European roses, 137–140, 152

'Excellenz von Schubert', **167**

Explorer series, 28, **144**, **165**

F

'Fairhope', 59

fertilizers and fertilizing, 27, 50, 67, 73, 151, 170–174

'First Prize', **14**, 47, 122

'Fisherman's Friend', **76**, 87

Floribunda roses, 28, **30**, **33**, 47, **56**, **59**, 71, 73, 94, 104, 107, **107**, 130. *See also specific Floribundas*

Florida, 36–41

'Flutterbye', 130

Follette, Charles, 108–113, **112**, 172–173

forget-me-not, 130

Fortuniana rootstock, 39, 170–171

'Fourth of July', 104

foxglove, 164, **167**

fragrance, 44, 81, 122, 127, 152

'Fragrant Cloud', **167**

'François Coppée', **139**

'French Lace', **33**, 104

French roses, 61

Furman, John, 104–107

G

gardenia, 36, 81

'Garden Party', 122

garden plans, 175–181

'Gene Boerner', **33**, 47

Geranium sanguineam 'Album' (cranesbill), 159

'Giggles', **59**

'Gold Medal', 47

'Gourmet Popcorn', 117

'Grace de Monaco', **121**

'Graham Thomas', **50**, **91**

Grandifloras, 25, 27, **27**, 54. *See also specific Grandifloras*

grasses and sedges, 19, **87**, **102**, 104, 107, **107**, 125, **126**

'Green Rose', 64, 67, **67**

Griffith Buck roses, 71

ground cover roses, **18**, 22, **116**, 117, **165**

growing tips, 170–174

Gypsophila spp. (baby's breath), 62, **62**, 164

H

Halsted, Steve and Carole, **102**, 130–135

'Hamburger Phoenix', **30**, 31

'Hebe's Lip', 127